GARY SOBERS'
MOST MEMORABLE
MATCHES

Gary Sobers' Most Memorable Matches

Gary Sobers

with Tony Cozier

Stanley Paul
London Melbourne Sydney Auckland Johannesburg

Stanley Paul & Co. Ltd

An imprint of the Hutchinson Publishing Group

17–21 Conway Street, London W1P 6JD

Hutchinson Publishing Group (Australia) Pty Ltd
PO Box 496, 16–22 Church Street, Hawthorne, Melbourne,
Victoria 3122

Hutchinson Group (NZ) Ltd
32–34 View Road, PO Box 40–086, Glenfield, Auckland 10

Hutchinson Group (SA) Pty Ltd
PO Box 337, Bergvlei 2012, South Africa

First published 1984
© Gary Sobers and Tony Cozier 1984

Set in Linotron Baskerville
by Input Typesetting Ltd, London

Printed and bound in Great Britain by Anchor Brendon Ltd,
Tiptree, Essex

British Library Cataloguing in Publication Data
Sobers, Gary
  Gary Sobers' most memorable matches.
  I. Sobers, Gary
  I. Title   II. Cozier, Tony
  796.35'8'0924   GV915.S6

ISBN 0 09 156300 3

Photographic Acknowledgements

For permission to reproduce copyright photographs, the publishers
would like to thank Patrick Eagar, the Press Association Ltd,
and Sport and General Press Agency Ltd.

Contents

Contents

Introduction

Venture into any cricket dressing room, into any bar where there are cricketers and cricket followers, and you're sure to find the conversation spiced with memories of great games, great deeds, great players of the past. Much of it will be sheer exaggeration as one particular delivery, say, from Lindwall or Hall or Trueman gets faster year by year as does the six hit by Kanhai or Dexter get longer and the catch by Cowdrey or Constantine get more dazzling.

Personally, I have a flood of memories from my many happy days on the grounds of the world. I count myself fortunate to have played this great game, which has brought me so many lasting friends and which has afforded me the opportunity to leave a few moments to be remembered by.

Trying to choose a limited number which I could honestly say were my 'most memorable' is a little like watching those beauty contests on television and trying to pick the favourites. In the end, you've got to leave out several that you know were worth inclusion.

However, it's been fun compiling this book, jogging the memory after all these years. *Wisden* and a few other reference books have come in very handy to make sure that I've not overstated the case, as we tend to do after the sun has set on our playing days!

You'll see that the matches span a period of twenty-one years and cover all kinds of cricket. The scientists haven't yet come up with a time machine which would allow me to do it all over again – but memory is the next best thing. I enjoyed it all and I hope you'll enjoy these matches with me too.

1 The Undersized 'Policeman'

Police v Empire and Wanderers, Bridgetown, 1952

The year 1952 has particularly vivid memories for me. It was the time when I first played in the top club league in Barbados, when my career as a budding 'Satchmo' Armstrong came to an abrupt end and when I scored my maiden century.

Cricket – in fact, any ball game – had been my life from the earliest days I can remember at our modest little bungalow in Walcott's Avenue in the Bayland, just outside Bridgetown. It seemed that myself, my brother Gerry and the boys from the area were always bowling, batting or kicking around a ball and my mum used to have a devil of a time getting us home for meals.

In the middle of the district was the Bay Pasture, famous as the headquarters of the Wanderers Cricket Club which had produced a number of outstanding players for Barbados and the West Indies. At the time, it was a very exclusive club but, even though we knew we wouldn't get into its membership, we enjoyed going there to watch Wanderers play in the Division One league of the Barbados Cricket Association and to bowling in the nets during the week.

For me, it was a great experience since Wanderers had such outstanding players as the Atkinson brothers, Denis and Eric, the Marshall brothers, Roy and Norman – all of whom played Test cricket eventually – along with a few Barbados island players as well. Perhaps it was because I was so small, but I got the impression I was a favourite and there was plenty of encouragement all round.

My own competitive cricket, however, was confined to the

Barbados Cricket League which catered for the less well-off clubs, mainly in the country areas. I had to play for a team out in the country with the delightful name of Penny Hole. The Bayland team, known as the Nationals, wouldn't pick me because they said I was too small. Maybe I was, and I looked even smaller in short pants, but all I wanted to do was to play. So when Garnet Ashby brought his team down from Penny Hole to play a friendly match in the Bayland, and when he saw me bowl and asked if I wanted to play with his team in the League, nothing could have stopped me. Well, perhaps Mum – but she gave it her okay and that's how I first got into a competitive team.

I did well enough for Penny Hole in the first season, 1951, when I was just turned fifteen, and I gained selection for the League's combined country team to play against a combined Bridgetown team which included my brother Gerry, a really good bat. There was quite a furore when I got him out in the match and I picked up some more wickets as well. As a result I was chosen in the overall League team for the big annual match against the Association's combination.

The Association usually won but, for the players from the League, it was an opportunity to move up the ladder, to be spotted by one of the better-known clubs. That's the way Test players like Seymour Nurse, Clairemonte dePeiza, Everton Weekes and Vanburn Holder made the breakthrough, and it happened with me as well.

I bowled pretty well, line and length with a little variation, and beat one of the Association's batsmen, Wilfred Farmer, a few times. Now 'Fee', as he was called by everyone, was Assistant Commissioner of Police at the time, a player good enough to have scored 275 for Barbados against Jamaica, and afterwards he asked me if I was interested in playing cricket for Police.

It was a real break but I couldn't understand how a little stripling, fifteen years of age at the time, could become a policeman just like that. Captain Farmer had the answer: 'You're a bit small so we'll have to let you try out for the band.' Lo and behold, a week later, I was a recruit in the Royal Barbados Police Force Band, learning how to 'lip' and blow the bugle!

My stay was to be short. My first match for Police was against Empire, one of the strongest and most famous clubs in Barbados, at their ground at Bank Hall. They say they use candlegrease to prepare the pitch and, in those days, it was as fast as any I've ever played on. Some of the great West Indies fast bowlers of all time – Herman Griffith and Manny Martindale in the 1930s and Charlie Griffith of more recent vintage – came through Empire and no wonder!

That day, they had in their side E.A.V. 'Foffie' Williams, who played Tests against England in 1935, 1939 and 1948 and who, even though he was then thirty-eight, was still fit and quick enough. I came in six or seven when we were in trouble and must have been playing quite easily when they took the second new ball at 200 and handed it to Foffie. In his first over, he went back to his mark, made a menacing sign by passing his index finger across his throat and, from a short run, let me have a bouncer. I picked it up late and wham, it caught me flush on the jaw.

I'd never been hit before and it was quite a shock, although I didn't fall and lose consciousness. Even so, I left the field and didn't bat again that innings. I could almost hear the Bayland people who had refused to play me in the Nationals team saying, 'I told you so.'

By the end of play, my jaw had become stiff and swollen and I knew that playing the bugle would be out for a few days. I sent a message to the band director, an Englishman by the name of Captain Raison, that I would be away for a couple of days but when I returned, he wasn't amused. 'I can see you're not really interested in music, young man,' he said, and if that wasn't strictly correct, the truth was that I was interested in cricket more and, then and there, Police Band recruit G. St A. Sobers disbanded, so to speak.

But Captain Farmer, with whom I grew to have a close personal relationship before his death at a sadly early age, wasn't going to let me go. The police force had, just then, formed a special boys' club less than a mile from our home. I was a member and the BCA agreed that a club member could play for Police until he became over-age. In fact, I continued playing for Police, without let or hindrance, throughout my career although other international commitments limited my future appearances. It's an association I've never regretted. After all, it's always best to be on the right side of the law!

The blow from Foffie Williams, happy to say, had no adverse side effects, physical or psychological and, later that season, having just turned sixteen, I scored my first-ever century. I'll never forget it for several reasons, primarily because it was against Wanderers at the Bay Pasture, a club I'd come to respect on a ground I knew so well. What is more, we were in all sorts of trouble. They made plenty, with a century from Denis Atkinson and we were 160-odd for seven when Carl Mullins, the fast bowler and a very good one too, joined me. Well, as the Wanderers players became more and more frustrated, we added about 170 and I passed my century. All my friends from the Bayland were there, seemingly happier even than I was, and it was quite a moment.

Little was I to know it at the time but, later in my career, I was to have close relationships with several of the Wanderers in that match. I played Test cricket with Denis and Eric Atkinson, and Norman Marshall, and I was West Indies captain when Noel Peirce, the Wanderers' skipper in those days, became President of the West Indies Cricket Board of Control.

I still value that century as highly as many of the others I've been fortunate to make in the years that have followed.

Captain Wilfred Farmer of the Barbados Police team, 1952: 'Talent such as that displayed by the young Sobers is so immediately impressive, so blatantly obvious to the eye of anyone with the merest grain of cricketing knowledge, that its early revelation to a

Police v Empire and Wanderers, Bridgetown, 1952

Police

F. Taylor	b Atkinson	11	c St Hill b R. Lawless	55
C. Blackman	c Mayers b Atkinson	46	b Atkinson	42
C. Aimey	c Toppin b Atkinson	5	c and b R. Lawless (6)	8
W. Farmer	c D. Lawless b Atkinson	59	run out (4)	0
J. Byer	c Atkinson b St Hill	14	c R. Lawless b Atkinson	2
A. Blenman	not out	3	c and b R. Lawless (3)	16
G. St A. Sobers	st Knowles b St Hill	0	not out	113
B. Dodson	c Knowles b St Hill	0	b Atkinson	17
C. Springer	b Atkinson	9	b Proverbs	35
C. Mullins	b St Hill	0	not out	67
C. Bradshaw	run out	1		
Extras		8		12
Total		**156**	(for 8 wickets declared)	**367**

Wanderers

W. Knowles	c Sobers b Mullins	77	b Mullins	1
D. Evelyn	c Mullins b Sobers	55	b Bradshaw	0
G. Proverbs	lbw b Mullins	7	not out	65
D. Atkinson	c Byer b Blackman	115		
M. Mayers	c Dodson b Mullins	1	not out	18
D. Lawless	b Mullins	5		
L. St Hill	b Mullins	11		
R. Lawless	b Mullins	53		
H. Toppin	b Mullins	0		
H. Ramsay	not out	0		
Extras		16		10
Total	(9 wickets declared)	**340**	(2 wickets)	**94**

Wanderers	O	M	R	W	O	M	R	W
Atkinson	24	7	64	5	37	7	108	3
Skeete	3	0	6	0	5	1	18	0
Lawless	4	0	29	0	13	1	83	3
Toppin	8	0	21	0	5	1	30	0
St Hill	13	1	27	4	21	5	70	0
Ramsay	1	0	1	0				
Knowles					7	0	18	0
Proverbs					3	0	14	1
Evelyn					2	0	14	0
Police								
Bradshaw	9	0	34	0	7	4	21	1
Mullins	25	3	93	7	6	1	14	1
Taylor	2	0	12	0	3	0	21	0
Sobers	20	2	80	1				
Byer	2	0	18	0				
Blackman	2.3	0	28	1				
Farmer	3	0	33	0				
Springer					3	0	21	0

wondering world was inevitable. The ability consistently to drive a tennis ball sizzlingly along the turf, to cut with absolute precision and to execute a series of sophisticated, if traditional, shots, mark a lad of thirteen with the stamp of genius for all to see and it becomes only a question of how soon.

'As luck would have it, I happened to see him at this age. The story has been told many times and Gary himself has related the occasion. If anything I did at the time was helpful to him, I'm naturally elated. But anyone else would have done the same. Fate, in her usual haphazard fashion, was merely being kind to this one of her wayward puppets.

'On that fateful Friday afternoon at the old Wanderers ground, Bayland, after Denis Atkinson and I had watched the miracle unfold for long enough to be conscious of the wonder, I enquired of a fan, Mr Tom Sealy, the identity of the prodigy. He told me, adding that he was the terror of the soft-ball games with bat and ball. I asked him to invite the youngster for a chat.

'It was then that it became immediately even more obvious that here was a boy of promise. He was shy, yes, but there was none of the usual shrinking, simpering, tongue-tied, hand-wringing reticence about him. He answered questions and volunteered information frankly and firmly. He bore himself manfully – not by any means mannishly – and met your eyes squarely and directly, with no trace of suspicion or defiance.

'And this has been Gary ever since. In the years immediately following, playing together for the Police Cricket Club, I got to know him better and to value him as a person even more highly.'

(Reproduced from Sobers Benefit Tournament Souvenir Brochure, April 1973.)

2 My First-Class Debut

Barbados v India, Bridgetown, 1953

It's not unusual to find teenagers in first-class West Indies cricket and even in Test sides. Derek Sealy played in his first Test when he was seventeen, Jeffrey Stollmeyer went to England in 1939 as a schoolboy, Clyde Walcott and Roy Marshall played for Barbados when they were fifteen.

The secret is that, in those days, the leading secondary schools played in the top division in club cricket so that the boys were put to the test early on and could show what they were worth. In my case, however, I didn't go to any of the top schools in Barbados and was fortunate to make my way into the Barbados team at the age of sixteen playing for Police – when I wasn't even a policeman.

You'll remember the previous chapter on my first season for Police. Well, after that blow on the jaw from Foffie Williams, I recovered to do pretty well, really, getting wickets as a left-arm spinner and some runs too, including that century against Wanderers.

The Barbados cricket season runs from early June until early December and is then followed by the first-class season from January until late April or early May. In other words, if you're good enough, you play cricket of one sort or another all the year round.

At the end of 1952, my own interest was whether I would be included in the list of players to take part in the Barbados trial matches for the first tour of the West Indies by India. Barbados would play only one match against them and places in the final eleven would be at a premium. But if I were

15

included in the trials, I knew those who mattered were taking some notice. As it turned out, I was among the 26 named, but the challenge was to be even harder than I might have expected.

The procedure was that the 'probables' would play the 'possibles' – in other words, the big guns would be all on one side, while the rest of us would be no more than sacrificial lambs. Perhaps it was a good thing for me, since I was able to bowl at batsmen like Clyde Walcott, Everton Weekes, Roy Marshall and Denis Atkinson. If they hit me all over the ground, it was only to be expected. If I held my own, it would be one up for me. I had nothing to lose – and I didn't. I kept it tight without turning much, picked up some wickets and, when the squad was announced for the match against the Indians at the end of January, I was in the twelve.

I thought at the time that it might just have been a little encouragement to a promising youngster and perhaps it was. But fate then took a hand. Also in the twelve was Frank King, one of the few genuine fast bowlers the West Indies then possessed (yes, there was a time when we were short of them) and he had bowled plenty in the first Test in Trinidad. When it was over, the West Indies selectors asked Barbados to give King a rest so that the way was clear for me to make my first-class debut. It left the team a little unbalanced, with only one genuine pacer, and two orthodox left-arm spinners in myself and Horace King. That was a few years before I took to bowling quick!

Now I look back on it, I really moved rapidly up the ladder in that one year since Captain Wilfred Farmer helped me get into the police band so that I could play cricket for the force. Now, here I was, not yet seventeen, representing Barbados against India alongside some of the greats of all time.

It was to be some while before I actually got to do anything, since we batted first and I watched from the pavilion as Everton Weekes helped himself to a typically brilliant double century. I did get a hand towards the end and when skipper John Goddard declared I was 7 not out and Barbados were

606 for seven! I said the batting was strong and I wasn't there to bat. I was picked as a left-arm spinner.

We had batted almost to the end of the second day of the five day match – and now had to field for the remaining three. We managed to get the Indians out for just over 200 but they had a fair batting team themselves and they just managed to hold out for a draw – thanks to rain and our ground staff. Even though it might have meant victory to Barbados, they couldn't bring themselves to go out into the downpour to cover the pitch. The Indians were nine wickets down at the time and almost certainly would have been beaten. But they say we West Indians run *to* a fire but run *away* from rain and we could do nothing about it!

My personal recollections of that match are of bowling and bowling and bowling – and picking up seven wickets as batsmen played for turn which wasn't there. Now I look back at the scorecard I see I had four for 50 in the first innings from 22 overs and then, in the second innings as India reached 445 for nine: 67 overs, 35 maidens, three for 92. Yes, I was young and fit then but I still get tired even thinking of it now!

What I do remember distinctly was that several batsmen went to the straight ball or the one with the arm. The scorecard confirms it – four bowled and the other three leg before.

The one that gave me the greatest pleasure was that of the great Indian player, Polly Umrigar. He was in when John Goddard brought me into the attack in the first innings with India struggling at a few for three. In my second over he picked up a ball on legstump and hit it onto the roof of the Kensington Stand at mid-wicket. I can tell you it was a bit of a shock but it had the effect of making me even more determined to get him out. I did, eventually, with one that went between bat and pad to bowl him for 60-odd. It was my first wicket in first-class cricket – and what a wicket!

I felt so good after that game that I was even half expecting a place in the Test team, especially when Sonny Ramadhin was unfit and couldn't play in the last Test in Jamaica. Oh, the confidence of youth. I wasn't even seventeen yet and I was itching to get into Test cricket. For that I would have to wait a little longer.

Barbadian author Gordon Bell: 'This was his biggest break up until then and he meant to take full advantage of it. In spite of some good performances with the bat he knew that it was as a left arm spin bowler that he had been chosen. As was to be expected he felt a bit nervous when his captain threw him the ball to begin his first over.

'Facing him was Polly Umrigar, a stylish batsman and hard-hitter who smashed the second ball from Garfield over the stands for six. This naturally upset Garfield but did not break his heart. Two balls later he completely mystified the batsman and clean bowled him. The roar of applause that greeted his first 'colony' wicket was sweet music to his ear and a tonic to his spirit. He was destined to receive applause like this and greater in the four corners of the cricketing world.'

(Reproduced from *Sir Garfield Sobers*, 1978.)

Barbados v India, Bridgetown, 1953

Barbados

R. E. Marshall	run out	25
C. C. Hunte	c Maka b Kannaiyaram	29
C. L. Walcott	c Phadkar b Hazare	51
E. D. Weekes	b Roy	253
C. B. Williams	c Umrigar b Phadkar	60
D. Atkinson	b Roy	81
J. D. Goddard	not out	50
C. dePeiza	b Gadkari	26
G. St A. Sobers	not out	7
Extras		24
Total	(7 wickets declared)	**606**

H. King and H. Barker did not bat.

India

P. Roy	lbw b Barker	4	c and b Atkinson	89
M. L. Apte	b Marshall	5	b Barker	4
V. L. Manjrekar	lbw b Marshall	44	lbw b Sobers	154
V. S. Hazare	c dePeiza b Barker	15	b Barker	38
P. R. Umrigar	b Sobers	63	not out	96
D. H. Phadkar	b Sobers	7	b Sobers	2
D. K. Gaekwad	lbw b Sobers	27	b Sobers	13
D. H. Shodhan	lbw b Sobers	0	run out	0
C. V. Gadkari	b Barker	24	c Walcott b Barker	9
E. S. Maka	b Marshall	9	c Walcott b King	9
N. Kannaiyaram	not out	10	not out	10
Extras		11	Extras	21
Total		**219**	(9 wickets)	**445**

India	O	M	R	W		O	M	R	W
Phadkar	40	8	98	1					
Kannaiyaram	18	2	60	1					
Shodhan	20	2	87	0					
Gadkari	35	2	154	1					
Hazare	20	1	85	1					
Manjrekar	6	0	30	0					
Gaekwad	1	0	10	0					
Roy	14	1	58	2					

Barbados	O	M	R	W		O	M	R	W
Barker	17.2	4	22	3		43	8	113	3
Atkinson	12	6	14	0		46	24	62	1
Marshall	29	8	62	3		26.4	6	77	0
King	12	4	29	0		15	5	34	1
Sobers	22	5	50	4		67	35	92	3
Walcott	9	5	13	0		17	7	27	0
Goddard	3	0	8	0		4	2	6	0
Weekes						9	3	13	0

3 My First Test
West Indies v England, Kingston, 1954

Ask a hundred cricketers about their first Test match, one of the highlights of their careers, and you'll probably get a hundred different answers. I've known players who couldn't recall one innings from another and others who could recite a particular century or bowling spell chapter and verse. Some remember little things, like what they had for breakfast, or the name of the movie they saw the night before, or the type of bat they used.

I still have a general picture in my mind's eye of my own Test debut, but without many incidents in particular detail. It was, after all, more years ago than I would care to admit! My most vivid recollection is of how I first heard I'd been selected for the final Test of the 1954 series against England at Sabina Park in Jamaica. As usual, the boys from the Bayland area of Bridgetown where I grew up were playing cricket in the street on Walcott's Avenue when Ben Hoyos, secretary of the Barbados Cricket Association, gave me the news.

'We've got a cable from the West Indies Board asking us to advise you to get ready to go to Jamaica,' he said. 'Seems as if Valentine is still not fit.' Tell that to the average cricket-mad seventeen-year-old and the reaction, I'm sure, would be the same as mine. My heart beat faster and all sorts of things flashed through my mind. Here I was, a teenager in short pants, playing cricket with my brothers and friends from the Bayland, being told I was wanted by the West Indies to play along with the three Ws, Walcott, Weekes and Worrell,

Ramadhin, Stollmeyer, and other greats in a Test against England with Hutton, May, Compton, Graveney, Evans, Laker, Lock and Trueman.

It wasn't that I was overawed. Even at that early age, I felt confident playing any ball game. I'd had a good grounding in Barbados club cricket, which is of a high standard, had proven myself the previous season in my first match for Barbados against the touring Indians and had again done reasonably well against the Englishmen in their match against Barbados early in the tour. True. But Test cricket was something else, the highest standard possible. Would it be that different? I couldn't wait to find out.

It's strange, but my first breaks both for Barbados and for the West Indies came because someone else pulled out. In the first instance, the fast bowler Frank King was rested by the selectors in the match against India in 1953 and now Val was unable to play in this Test. Not that I minded!

It may sound strange as well in this day and age that when I left Barbados in late March 1954, bound for Jamaica and the Test, it was the first time I'd ever left the island, the first time I'd ever flown in a plane. It was all happening, as they say – although subsequently, as far as travelling is concerned, I have certainly made up for the late start.

First impressions, of course, are usually the most lasting and I believe the close affinity which I was to have with Sabina Park and the crowds there in future years developed on that first trip. It was so different from Kensington Oval, with its very short straight boundaries, its wooden stands, its huge pavilion and the beauty of the Blue Mountain range as the backdrop to the northern end. In two respects there were similarities: the pitch, hard and true, and the crowd, noisy, involved and informed.

It was an important match, since we held a 2–1 lead and only needed to draw to clinch the rubber. When we won the toss and Jeffrey Stollmeyer, our captain, told me he had put me in at No. 9, I settled back to watch the current heroes of

21

West Indies cricket bat. I certainly didn't expect to get in too soon.

How wrong I was. In fact I found myself padding up even before lunch as Trevor Bailey played havoc with our early batting. I went in with seven down for 110. Naturally, I was a little tense, which is not a bad thing since it makes you concentrate. But I can't say I was nervous in the sense that I had butterflies or that I was mentally confused. Naturally there was no real pressure, since I was in primarily for my left-arm spin bowling and not my batting, but I still wanted to prove what I could do. The match brochure listed me as a 'useful' batsman. I wanted to prove I was a little more than that!

Bailey and Freddie Trueman were bowling when I came in and, without wanting to sound in any way precocious, I really couldn't understand why we had collapsed as we did, for the pitch and the light were perfect. I got 14 and then, for one of the few times in my Test career (despite what the critics say), I ran out of partners!

So far, so good and, even though the dressing room was understandably glum when I got back in, everyone made the teenaged newcomer feel as if he'd made a century debut, rather than a modest 14 not out! We were back in the field before the day was out and, early next day, Jeff Stollmeyer called me up for my first bowl. He had tried Frank King and Gerry Gomez with the new ball and then Denis Atkinson and Sonny Ramadhin without success when he brought the teenaged Sobers on. Lo and behold, in my first over (I have an idea it was the fourth ball), Trevor Bailey attempted a cut and was caught behind by Cliff McWatt. I honestly can't remember very much about the delivery although I suppose, being my first Test wicket and all, I should. Trevor, who later became a close personal friend and wrote my biography, says he was playing for turn and it was only afterwards that he discovered I didn't turn!

It was my last success for some time since Hutton batted magnificently for a double century which just about sealed

West Indies v England, Kingston, 1953–54 (5th Test)

West Indies

J. K. Holt	c Lock b Bailey	0	c Lock b Trueman	8
J. B. Stollmeyer*	c Evans b Bailey	9	lbw b Trueman	64
E. de C. Weekes	b Bailey	0	b Wardle	3
F. M. M. Worrell	c Wardle b Trueman	4	c Graveney b Trueman	29
C. L. Walcott	c Laker b Lock	50	c Graveney b Laker	116
D. St E. Atkinson	lbw b Bailey	21	c Watson b Bailey (7)	40
G. E. Gomez	c Watson b Bailey	4	lbw b Laker (6)	22
C. A. McWatt†	c Lock b Bailey	22	c Wardle b Laker	8
G. St A. Sobers	not out	14	c Compton b Lock	26
F. M. King	b Bailey	9	not out (11)	10
S. Ramadhin	lbw b Trueman	4	c and b Laker (10)	10
Extras	(LB 1, NB 1)	2	(B 4, LB 3, W 1, NB 2)	10
Total		**139**		**346**

England

L. Hutton*	c McWatt b Walcott	205		
T. E. Bailey	c McWatt b Sobers	23		
P. B. H. May	c sub (B. H. Pairaudeau) b Ramadhin	30	not out	40
D. C. S. Compton	hit wkt b King	31		
W. Watson	c McWatt b King	4	not out (2)	20
T. W. Graveney	lbw b Atkinson	11	b King (1)	0
T. G. Evans†	c Worrell b Ramadhin	28		
J. H. Wardle	c Holt b Sobers	66		
G. A. R. Lock	b Sobers	4		
J. C. Laker	b Sobers	9		
F. S. Trueman	not out	0		
Extras	(LB 3)	3	(B 12)	12
Total		**414**	(1 wicket)	**72**

England	O	M	R	W	O	M	R	W
Bailey	16	7	34	7	25	11	54	1
Trueman	15.4	4	39	2	29	7	88	3
Wardle	10	1	20	0	39	14	83	1
Lock	15	6	31	1	27	16	40	1
Laker	4	1	13	0	50	27	71	4

West Indies	O	M	R	W	O	M	R	W
King	26	12	45	2	4	1	21	1
Gomez	25	8	56	0				
Atkinson	41	15	82	1	3	0	8	0
Ramadhin	29	9	71	2	3	0	14	0
Sobers	28.5	9	75	4	1	0	6	0
Walcott	11	5	26	1				
Worrell	11	0	34	0	4	0	8	0
Stollmeyer	5	0	22	0				
Weekes					0.5	0	3	0

our fate in that game. But I did come back towards the end to finish off the innings with the wickets of those illustrious bowlers Johnnie Wardle, Tony Lock and Jim Laker, so that the figures – four for 75 – didn't look at all bad in my debut Test match. Even though I was picked as a bowler, however, I did fancy myself a bit with the bat and the fact that I got 26 in our second innings was even more satisfying than my bowling.

All things considered, it was a fair start. Little was I to know at the time that it would lead to quite so long a stay in Test cricket.

English writer E. W. Swanton: 'Before Ramadhin went, Sobers had been able to show several wristy left-hander's strokes and to make it clear furthermore than nothing Trueman could send down was too fast to ruffle him.'

'. . . Sobers made an excellent impression. He is a slim young man who runs lightly up to the wicket and the arm almost touches the ear as it comes over. On what might serve as a model action for a slow left-hand bowler, he builds changes of flight and spin in the classical manner. It will be surprising if we do not come to know his name well in the years ahead.'

(Reproduced from *Cricket From All Angles*.)

4 Opening Fire

West Indies v Australia, Bridgetown, 1955

Most of the memories contained in these pages deal with long innings and big scores. Now, for a change, something short and sweet: a score of 43 including ten fours, as an opening batsman in my fourth Test.

Let me put the occasion in perspective. The year was 1955 and the Australians were on their first tour of the West Indies and giving us a hard time. We had lost the first and third Tests to be down 2-0, and our cause wasn't helped by some strange decisions by the selectors. They dropped Collie Smith from the third Test after he had scored a debut century in the first and they managed to leave out both Ramadhin and Valentine at the same time for the third Test, although they had a late change of mind and recalled Ram when the pitch looked as if it might favour spin. In addition, there was controversy over the captaincy, whether it should go to Denis Atkinson, who took over from the injured Jeff Stollmeyer, or Frank Worrell.

Eccentric selection and controversy are no strangers to West Indies cricket but they were more in evidence that season than usual. We certainly could have done without such distractions against a strong Australian team led by Ian Johnson and including such class batsman as Neil Harvey, Arthur Morris and Colin McDonald along with the fast bowling of Ray Lindwall and Keith Miller and the all-round talents of a youthful Richie Benaud and Ron Archer.

When we arrived at Barbados, with two Tests remaining, the West Indies team had been chopped and changed so much and the captaincy argument was raging to such an extent that there was no way we could find the spirit to pull back from our two-game deficit.

I was then nineteen years of age, in my first full Test series and, while I didn't like being on a losing side, I was fully enjoying myself playing against the tough but sporting Aussies. Come the fourth Test, in typical West Indian fashion, we took the field with only one recognized opening batsman (J. K. Holt) after Jeffrey Stollmeyer was out with a leg injury sustained in the previous Test. Now, to play in any team without two specialist opening batsmen may seem a little strange against opponents for whom Lindwall and Miller, one of the greatest fast bowling combinations the game has known, share the new ball. But, as I said, anything was possible with the West Indies that season.

Ian Johnson won the toss, batted on the perfect Kensington Oval pitch and Australia piled up over 600 in their first innings with even Miller and Lindwall scoring centuries. The match was spread over six days and it was well into the third day before we got in. The question as to who might open with J. K. had been a juicy subject for the pressmen and it seemed as if Clairemonte dePeiza, our wicket-keeper, might get the job since he had done it (without much success, I might add) in the preceding Barbados match.

The subject didn't concern me, I felt. Well, I was wrong. Out of the blue, Denis Atkinson came up to me in the dressing-room between innings. 'You had better get the pads on, lad, you're going to open,' he said. Now I'd never opened the batting in any kind of cricket before and could only feel now that I was being used as a sacrifice since the three Ws – Walcott, Weekes and Worrell – were Nos. 3, 4, and 5 and could not be shifted, while dePeiza might have been tired after his long period behind the stumps. So I had nothing to lose and I decided as I walked down the pavilion steps that whenever I saw red I'd throw the bat. As a friend of mine used to say, 'I'm here for a good time, not a long time.'

Holt took strike for Lindwall's first over and I had to

handle Miller, fast, dynamic, unpredictable. In his first over I took three boundaries, the first a hook to fine leg, the second through the covers and the third a slash past point. 'Not bad,' I thought to myself. 'This is fun.'

Next over, I threw the bat again and had three more fours – all through the off-side, all whistling off the middle of the bat. In Keith's third over, I got another four, through the covers – seven fours in three overs. By then, the crowd was shouting and screaming and jumping all over the place. They couldn't believe that this little boy from the Bayland was attacking the great Miller in this fashion. To tell the truth, the little boy from the Bayland couldn't believe it either!

I had the impression that even the opposition was enjoying it slightly. When I was at the non-striker's end Ray Lindwall turned to me and, with a big smile on his face, said: 'Good going, son, but you stay at this end.' In fact, when Ray took the first wicket by yorking J.K. the total was 52, and we had not changed ends!

By the time I did get down to face Lindwall, I wanted to hit every ball for four and started by putting him away for my eighth boundary. By this time, Keith was out of the attack and soon Ian Johnson, bowling his flighted off-spin, came on. The temptation was too much. I swept him for my tenth four out of 43 (the other strokes were singles) and then went to sweep him again, of course hitting against the turn and whatever bounce he might get. The result was that I top-edged a catch to Jack Hill three-quarters of the way to the boundary at backward square leg.

It was a frantic innings and, as everybody knew, couldn't last forever. But to this day several of those who were there still talk about it when we get together in Barbados. It was that kind of innings and, even if it was only 43, it was something a little different, you might say. Ian Johnson also remembers it. When he sees me in Melbourne, where he has recently retired after many years as secretary of the Melbourne Cricket Club, he frequently teases me. 'Hey, there's my rabbit,' he says. 'You know you kept me in cricket longer than I should have been.'

That particular match, of course, is remembered much more for the magnificent, fighting, record seventh-wicket partnership of 347 between Denis Atkinson and Clairemonte dePeiza, which pulled us out of real trouble to help us to a draw. Denis got a double century and 'Deep' a century – the only three-figure innings either ever reached in Test cricket. It just showed what a little fighting spirit could do.

There's one story during that partnership which emphasizes the sporting way the Australians played their cricket on that tour. Denis went down the pitch during his innings to have a chat with dePeiza, thinking the ball was dead. It wasn't, and Keith Miller picked it up, walked to the stumps and said: 'You know I could run you out, Denis.' He was perfectly within his rights to do so – but he didn't.

Australian writer Pat Landsberg: ' . . . The West Indies needed 518 to avoid the follow-on. There was no other course open to them but to take desperate measures and the one they chose was to send in young Garfield Sobers with Holt. What immediate sensations were to be the result of this gamble – Sobers had never opened an innings in his life before – no one could possibly have seen. After Holt had opened his account with two off Lindwall, Sobers took seven fours in succession off Miller. Three came in the first over. One to fine-leg, a second a glorious punch through covers and the third, off the last ball, which shot past point like a typhoon. In the next over from Miller Sobers hit three more – past mid-off, past gully and through the covers. Holt took time out to hit Lindwall for four wide of Harvey at point before Sobers resumed his attack on Miller. But this time he took only one four, the favourite Harvey shot through the covers.'

(From *The Kangaroo Conquerors*.)

West Indies v Australia, Bridgetown, 1954–55 (4th Test)

Australia

C. C. McDonald	run out	46	b Smith	17
L. E. Favell	c Weekes b Atkinson	72	run out	53
R. N. Harvey	c Smith b Worrell	74	c Valentine b Smith	27
W. J. Watson	c dePeiza b Dewdney	30	b Atkinson	0
K. R. Miller	c dePeiza b Dewdney	137	lbw b Atkinson	10
R. Benaud	c Walcott b Dewdney	1	b Sobers	5
R. G. Archer	b Worrell	98	lbw b Atkinson	28
R. R. Lindwall	c Valentine b Atkinson	118	b Atkinson (9)	10
I. W. Johnson*	b Dewdney	23	c Holt b Smith (8)	57
G. R. A. Langley†	b Sobers	53	not out	28
J. C. Hill	not out	8	c Weekes b Atkinson	1
Extras	(B 1, LB 2, W4, NB 1)	8	(B 9, LB 4)	13
Total		**668**		**249**

West Indies

J. K. Holt	Lindwall	22	lbw b Hill	49
G. St A. Sobers	c Hill b Johnson	43	lbw b Archer	11
C. L. Walcott	c Langley b Benaud	15	b Benaud	83
E. de C. Weekes	c Langley b Miller	44	run out	6
F. M. M. Worrell	run out	16	c Archer b Miller	34
O. G. Smith	c Langley b Miller	2	b Lindwall	11
D. St E. Atkinson*	c Archer b Johnson	219	not out	20
C. C. dePeiza†	b Benaud	122	not out	11
S. Ramadhin	c and b Benaud	10		
D. T. Dewdney	b Johnson	0		
A. L. Valentine	not out	2		
Extras	(B 5, LB 4, W 2, NB 4)	15	(B 6, LB 2, W 1)	9
Total		**510**	(6 wickets)	**234**

West Indies	O	M	R	W	O	M	R	W
Worrell	40	7	120	2	7	0	25	0
Dewdney	33	5	125	4	10	4	23	0
Walcott	26	10	57	0				
Valentine	31	9	87	0	6	1	16	0
Ramadhin	24	3	84	0	2	0	10	0
Atkinson	48	14	108	2	36.2	16	56	5
Smith	22	8	49	0	34	12	71	3
Sobers	11.5	6	30	1	14	3	35	1

Australia	O	M	R	W	O	M	R	W
Lindwall	25	3	96	1	8	1	39	1
Miller	22	2	113	2	21	3	66	1
Archer	15	4	44	0	7	1	11	1
Johnson	35	13	77	3	14	4	30	0
Hill	24	9	71	0	11	2	44	1
Benaud	31.1	6	73	3	11	3	35	1
Harvey	4	0	16	0				
Watson	1	0	5	0				

5 The Best Beach Everton Had Seen

West Indies v England, the Oval, 1957

The first time I set foot on English soil was on a cold, grey April morning in 1957 when I arrived with the West Indies team aboard the SS *Golfito* at Southampton. It was our first tour of England since the historic 1950 triumph, when the West Indies had first shown the world they were a force to reckon with by their 3–1 victory in the Test series.

When I was a boy, growing up in the Bayland just outside of Bridgetown, England was the headquarters of cricket. We would read reports and hear the commentaries coming from Lord's or the Oval or Old Trafford and try to picture events. When we played our own games on the street with a soft ball, we pretended to be playing at those famous grounds – although somehow, we could never manage the kind of misty, damp mornings conjured up so often by John Arlott!

By this time, I had become an established member of the team and was naturally looking forward to playing in English conditions, which we had been told were so different from ours at home. A tour of New Zealand a year earlier was, according to those who had been to England before, just the type of experience needed. Since I had failed badly with the bat in New Zealand, I was a little apprehensive about how I would fare in England. I wasn't so worried about the team as a whole because it seemed, on paper, a very strong one and there was a lot of optimism at home that we would repeat the 1950 successes.

We knew England to be strong but we had what the cricket writers like to call a 'blend of youth and experience' – the

three Ws, plus Ramadhin and Valentine – the heroes of 1950 – along with young types like Rohan Kanhai, Collie Smith, Roy Gilchrist, Wes Hall and myself. For several reasons the blend didn't work. The most important reason was that we did not knit as a team. It was something I wasn't aware of all the time: at twenty-one I was interested only in playing the game. But it became pretty clear in later years and made me realize how a lack of team spirit could affect any team, no matter how good.

By the time we went into the final Test at the Oval we had already lost the series, beaten by an innings at both Lord's and Headingley in three days, and the fact that injury kept out two of our best bowlers, Valentine and Denis Atkinson, didn't help matters much.

Still, I was reasonably satisfied with my own performance. I had played more cricket in a concentrated period than I had ever done in my life; I made a double century at Nottingham where, as fate would have it, I would one day play county cricket, and my first knock at Lord's had yielded an unbeaten 101 against the MCC. And I was bowling a lot, even if I wasn't getting many wickets. I was young, I was playing almost every day of the week on England's magnificent grounds and enjoying it. Even if we had lost the series, we went through the county matches unbeaten.

It turned out to be a dry and mostly warm summer after the initiation to the chill of April and we encountered almost every type of pitch: from the celebrated green tops, to the beauties of Edgbaston and Trent Bridge, to the ridge at Lord's. When we arrived at the Oval for the final Test, however, we came across something I never experienced before or since

When we went out to bowl on the first day, the pitch came under close examination. It had a funny colour to it, a darkish pink is the way I remember it. But how would it play? It wasn't long before we found out. Frank Worrell and Tom Dewdney had a few exploratory overs with the new ball and then John Goddard tossed the ball to Ram and myself. 'I think it's going to break up,' he said, which was a pretty fair assumption after a few balls had brought up dust. And that in the first half-hour!

We just about knew what to expect from the second ball I bowled. It turned a foot, took the edge of David Sheppard's bat and flew between Gerry Alexander behind the wicket and Clyde Walcott at slip. I saw Clyde look at Everton and nod knowingly and then Everton raise his eyebrows to Frank. Perhaps they were surprised I actually got a ball to turn!

As it happened England scored 412 on that pitch although Ram, myself, John Goddard and Collie Smith bowled something like 150 overs between us, all of us spinners of one type or another. We might not have bowled as well as we should have in the conditions, but the turn on the first day was slow and I feel if we had had Val (who had been injured in the match before and could not play) and Denis Atkinson (who had been ill and out of action for a month), England wouldn't have made half as many since both Val and Denis were spinners who pushed the ball through.

England had two spinners, Jim Laker and Tony Lock by name, who were not exactly novices and who must have been licking their chops all through our innings. They complemented each other, Jim off-spin from a height and Lockie left-arm orthodox. As Surrey men this was their ground, and they must have known every blade of grass on it.

They had become one of the most famous bowling partnerships in the game and the season before, Jim had put his name in the record books with his nineteen wickets in a Test against Australia. If he had had *this* kind of pitch regularly, he might have set that record on many occasions.

We really didn't have a price and were bowled out for 89 and 86 as the pitch became progressively worse. The top went completely and Everton, always one for a wise crack even in adversity, said it was the best beach he had seen in England! In these circumstances, I got tremendous satisfaction from the two innings I played – 39 in the first, 42 in the second. Sometimes, you don't have to make a big score to know you've played well. This was such an occasion. I suppose I proved to myself then that I could play in difficult conditions, that I could put my nut down, graft and concentrate: that I didn't need to play strokes all the time.

It is no exaggeration to describe this as the worst Test pitch I've played on, in that it favoured slow to medium spinners to an unjustifiable extent. Only that at Sabina Park in 1968 was comparable, but of a completely different nature. A team including the three Ws, Kanhai and Collie Smith doesn't get bowled out for under 100 twice unless something is wrong. In our first innings, the last nine wickets fell for 21 in 35 minutes!

Lock had eleven wickets in the match and time and again in my innings made the ball turn and jump and hit me in the chest or on the arm as I played forward. Poor Nyron Asgarali, the opener from Trinidad who stayed a long time battling it out with me in both innings, got a ball from Lock in the second innings which pitched leg and hit the top of the off stump. Fielders were all around the bat like vultures.

I think I must have batted for about two hours in both innings but it felt like two days. I might have spoiled it by finally playing two big shots and being bowled by Lock each time. E. W. Swanton described it as 'a lapse into the agricultural', a phrase I remember because it brought some good-natured ribbing from some of the boys.

What gave me the greatest pleasure was a visit I received in the dressing room afterwards from a tall, distinguished-looking man. 'Well played, son,' he told me. 'I've watched you all this series and know you're a better batsman than a bowler. You proved it today, for it needed something special to bat the way you did on that wicket. You'll go from strength to strength, I'm sure of it.'

He was introduced to me as Frank Wooley, a name from the past I had vaguely heard of, arguably the finest England left-handed batsman of all time, a left-arm spin bowler and sharp close catcher. Perhaps he saw in the youthful Sobers a kindred spirit, for we met several times in later years before

England v West Indies, the Oval, 1957 (5th Test)

England

P. E. Richardson	b Smith	107
Rev. D. S. Sheppard	c and b Goddard	40
T. W. Graveney	b Ramadhin	164
P. B. H. May*	c Worrell b Smith	1
M. C. Cowdrey	b Ramadhin	2
T. E. Bailey	run out	0
T. G. Evans†	c Weekes b Dewdney	40
G. A. R. Lock	c Alexander b Sobers	17
F. S. Trueman	b Ramadhin	22
J. C. Laker	not out	10
P. J. Loader	lbw b Ramadhin	0
Extras	(B 1, LB 8)	9
Total		**412**

West Indies

F. M. M. Worrell	c Lock b Loader	4	c Cowdrey b Lock (4)	0
N. R. Asgarali	c Cowdrey b Lock	29	b Lock	7
G. St A. Sobers	b Lock	39	b Lock	42
C. L. Walcott	b Laker	5	not out (5)	19
E. de C. Weekes	c Trueman b Laker	0	b Lock (6)	0
O. G. Smith	c May b Laker	7	c Sheppard b Lock (7)	0
R. B. Kanhai	not out	4	c Evans b Trueman (1)	8
F. C. M. Alexander†	b Lock	0	b Laker	0
D. T. Dewdney	b Lock	0	st Evans b Lock	1
S. Ramadhin	c Trueman b Lock	0	b Laker	2
J. D. C. Goddard*	absent ill	–	absent ill	–
Extras	(NB 1)	1	(B 4, LB 2, NB 1)	7
Total		**89**		**86**

West Indies	O	M	R	W	O	M	R	W
Worrell	11	3	26	0				
Dewdney	15	2	43	1				
Ramadhin	53.3	12	107	4				
Sobers	44	6	111	1				
Goddard	23	10	43	1				
Smith	30	4	73	2				

England	O	M	R	W	O	M	R	W
Trueman	5	1	9	0	5	2	19	1
Loader	7	4	12	1	3	2	2	0
Laker	23	12	39	3	17	4	38	2
Lock	21.4	12	28	5	16	7	20	6

he moved to live, I believe, in Canada where he died at the ripe old age of ninety-one.

'Strength to strength,' he had said. Well, you might say that he was right – although I was glad I didn't have to bat on any more pitches like the one at the Oval in 1957.

English writer E. W. Swanton: '. . . No cricketer present at the Oval would maintain that this sort of wicket which puts such an enormous premium on the possession of a slow-medium spinner – Lock bowled practically at medium pace for much of the time and all through was accordingly more difficult to play than Laker – and which makes stroke-making so extraordinarily hazardous except against the short-pitched ball, is the proper surface on which to contest a Test match in fine weather.

'The fact is that the shocking heresy about preparing wickets in order to help the bowlers and so ensure a finish in county cricket has got such a hold that the art of preparing a plumb wicket on which a bowler has to stretch his skill, his wits and his stamina to get his reward seems in danger of being lost.'

(Reproduced from the *Daily Telegraph*,
Monday, 26 August 1957.)

6 A Flipper in My League

Radcliffe v Oldham, Radcliffe, 1958

There has been no cricket in my experience quite like cricket in the Lancashire Leagues. Before the county scene opened up to overseas players in the late 1960s, the leagues in the Lancashire area – and especially the Lancashire League and the Central Lancashire League – provided the opportunity for some of the great international players to make the game their living by being attached to the clubs on a professional basis during the English summer.

Before the war, players like the legendary Learie Constantine, Manny Martindale, George Headley and Puss Achong blazed a trail into the Lancashire leagues for West Indian players which those of us after the war followed in large numbers. And not only West Indians: Australians, Indians, Pakistanis, New Zealanders and South Africans were all there too, including some of the greatest players the game has known.

Why did we go? First of all, it was the only cricket being played at that time of year in which the professional could earn his keep. Secondly, and equally important, it broadened our cricket education, teaching us how to play in different conditions and how to accept responsibility.

The matter of responsibility was crucial. I first went into the Central Lancashire League in 1958, after my first tour of England, to take the place of Frank Worrell at that famous old club, Radcliffe. I had heard West Indian players who had been in the leagues for some time talk with enthusiasm about

37

their experiences and Frank left me in no doubt as to what was expected.

'You're the number one,' he told me. 'They expect the pro to do everything. The success of the side depends on how well you do.' The arrangement, in fact, was that the pro was the one Test or first-class player in a team otherwise comprising amateurs, some good, some not so good, some who had been there for years, others, youngsters with promise who might catch the attention of a county by their performances.

My very first match was against Oldham at Radcliffe and a few days before, while I was at home with Frank and his lovely wife Velda, Frank said: 'Oh, you'll find an Australian in the Oldham team, name of Cec Pepper. A real top pro. He's been here for years and knows the ropes. He's a tremendous, hard-hitting batsman and a leg-spinner but for heaven's sake, don't let him do you with his "flipper". It's the best in the business, so watch for it.'

Cec was something of a legend in the leagues but I was the one who was on trial in that match. A big crowd turned out to see just what their new young signing would do. They followed their league cricket very keenly in those days and were extremely knowledgeable. If you failed, they wanted to know why.

We won the toss and I asked the captain if I could bat at No. 4, since it was my first game. In many cases, the pro was expected to open both batting and bowling but I wanted to have a look first. It wasn't long before Cec was on and it wasn't long either before he knocked our first two over. So in I went, fortunately getting in at the opposite end so I could watch a bit before I faced the bowler Frank had warned me about. When I did face Cec, I kept drumming in my head: 'watch for the flipper', 'don't play back'.

For a few overs, I kept watchful but old Cec was no fool. He knew Frank would have had a talk with me and knew I would have been forewarned about his most lethal ball. So he bided his time. I passed 20 and then 30 and there was still no sign of that flipper, the one that skids through in a flash.

By now, I had been in for a half-hour or so and was beginning to relax. Cec saw his chance and let me have it. My eyes must have opened like saucers when I saw what I thought to be a long hop and I went back to pull. Suddenly, in a twinkling, the warning lights flashed. 'Flipper' they said and I just froze there, keeping my bat down and just blocking the ball as it skidded through straight for the stumps. I must have looked horribly awkward but at least I was still there.

Startled, Cec walked down the pitch. 'That so-and-so Worrell's been talking to you, hasn't he?' and he went back muttering one or two more invectives.

He was a typical Australian, a tough competitor on the field but a great friend off it and we had many memorable duels after that. He was one of only two players to have scored 1000 runs and taken over 100 wickets in the Lancashire League before switching over to Central Lancashire.

I asked Cec just how he managed to get the ball to skid off the pitch like he did for that change ball. Some time afterwards I faced Richie Benaud, another great leg-spinner with a dangerous 'flipper', but even his didn't have the pace off the pitch that Cec's did. His secret was that he had massive hands and he used the palm in his delivery, almost like squeezing out a bar of soap.

Apart from his advice about Pepper, Frank Worrell also gave me two other hints on league cricket. The first was about the ritual of the collection. While all the pros were paid a basic fee, we could considerably boost our pay by performance. On a batsman reaching 50, club members would go around the ground with collection boxes and the crowd would 'show their appreciation', as they used to say, with a shilling or two or more, in some cases. The same thing would happen when someone passed 100 or took five or more wickets.

Frank's words on this score had behind them several seasons of experience. 'Now don't do anything foolish when you've passed 50 just because it means you've got your

collection,' he said. 'If you get out when the collection is being taken you won't raise another penny. Wait until you can hear the last coin dropped in and can see the boxes being taken away: you can do what you like after that!' It was great advice and the system proved a tremendous incentive to all the pros. Frank also told me that I wouldn't find people anywhere who loved their cricket more, or who were as warm-hearted as the people around the league towns of Lancashire.

On Cec Pepper's 'flipper', the timing of the collection and on his assessment of the warmth of people in league cricket, Frank proved – as usual – to be spot on.

Sir Frank Worrell, former West Indies captain: 'One can learn more in three years of league cricket than in twelve years of cricket outside the UK, even at the international level. One learns to cope with the swerving ball, the turning ball, the cutter, the stopping ball. One has to be brave enough to ignore the cold, dark or blustery weather, the running noses, watery eyes, cold hands, cold feet (literally and figuratively), the sometimes faulty umpiring decisions, dropped catches and the traditional needle matches.

'The professional who can take these things in his stride will return to international cricket not only as an individual with something to subscribe to the game but, what is even more important, he will also have that extremely rare quality of knowing how to lose.

'One of the greatest assets one gets out of league cricket is a tremendous sense of responsibility.'

(From *Frank Worrell: The Career of a Great Cricketer* by Ernest Eytle, 1963.)

7 Breaking the Barrier

West Indies v Pakistan, Kingston, 1958

This is the story of how a century turned into a double century and then a triple and, eventually, into a world record.

It may sound strange in this day and age of constant Test cricket but I played only fourteen Tests in the first three years of my career and, in all those matches – starting with the single debut Test against England in 1954, then four against Australia in 1955, four more in New Zealand in 1956 and the full five in England in 1957 – I hadn't scored a century. I don't mind admitting that I was becoming a little anxious about it, not so much on my own account but because there were those who kept wondering if I really would fulfil my potential as a batsman at Test level.

Two of those closely involved with West Indies cricket at the time, the former Guyana and West Indies player and selector, Berkeley Gaskin, and the radio commentator, Roy Lawrence, often told me that all I needed was to break the barrier and the hundreds would flow after that. It was a useful theory, I suppose, if you remember what happened after Roger Bannister broke the four-minute mile.

When Pakistan came to the West Indies for their first tour – and our first series against each other – in 1958, I was really determined to make the breakthrough. I had scored centuries in inter-island cricket in the West Indies and on tour. So why not in the Tests?

Since I was last at home, I had played cricket in the Lancashire League with Frank Worrell's old club, Radcliffe, and this had been a tremendous experience. Most of the West

Indian greats of that time had contracts in league cricket, since county cricket was still pretty much a closed shop to overseas players who could only qualify through a long residential period. Frank, Everton Weekes and the others had always told me my cricketing education wasn't complete until I learned to play in all conditions, and the league certainly provided them. What is more, as I was the club professional, it heightened my sense of responsibility.

I felt it in my bones, when I returned home for that series, that this was the occasion to put to rest, once and for all, that bogey about a maiden Test century. I was batting better than I had ever done and *knew* it, which was even more important. My first innings against the Pakistanis was 183 not out for Barbados in the island match, yet, although I made a half-century in the first and followed that with another 50-odd and 81 in the second, the Test century remained elusive.

When we went on to Jamaica for the third Test I was more determined than ever to make a big score. The Pakistanis had two good new-ball bowlers in the great Fazal Mahmood, who wobbled the ball around and seldom bowled a bad ball, and a big fast-medium trundler by the name of Khan Mohammad. But it was hardly a devilish attack and, on the hard, fast pitch at Sabina Park, I said to myself: 'It's now or never!'

I went in to bat on the second afternoon after Pakistan were out for 328 and Rohan Kanhai, opening with Conrad Hunte, had gone fairly cheaply. I was the No. 3 in that series and someone up there seemed to have ordained that this was to be a batting feast for anyone who wanted to partake. The pitch, as usual, was a beauty. What is more, by the time I came in, Mahmood Hussein had so badly torn a muscle in the very first over of the match that he did not bowl another ball on tour and, soon, the left-arm spinner Nasim-ul-Ghani cracked his left thumb and was off the field as well after 14 overs.

This was one opportunity I wasn't going to let go. Neither, it seemed, was Conrad Hunte. He had made his Test debut in this series and made a century in his very first Test. Later, he was to become a very solid opening batsman who gave the West Indies innings stability at the top but, at this time, he was a stroke player. He certainly played his strokes in that innings and duly reached his century, his second in only his third Test. With great relief, I soon followed him to my maiden Test century but, to tell the truth, I can't remember much about it – the stroke, the bowler, the crowd reaction, anything.

I was concentrating too fiercely to have noticed, which was just as well. I am sure that if I had relaxed there would have been the temptation to give it away after passing the magic figure. As it was, I ended the third day of that six-day Test 226 not out and, for the first time in my life, spent a restless night. At the end of a day's play, before and since, I count myself lucky that I can completely relax and put the cricket out of my mind until we start again. Perhaps this time, with the intense concentration, the elation of my first Test century and, just possibly, the talk of records which was going around, I found myself tossing and turning in my hotel bed that night.

Not that I was concerned about records. I was just intent on batting on as I had been doing, because I really felt as if I could never get out. However, Conrad *was* thinking of a record and it was this which ended our partnership.

He told me when we went out from lunch on the fourth day that we were only a few runs short of some record partnership – as I discovered later 451 by Bradman and Ponsford against England for the overall Test fourth wicket mark – and we should aim to beat it. I couldn't understand why he didn't feel we would beat it batting as we had done and, trying to get the single which he thought would break the record, he pushed to midwicket, took off and was run out by a direct throw at the bowler's end.

What a waste, I thought, for Conrad had 260 in the book and was seeing the ball as big as a breadfruit. Later, we learned he had mistaken the figure and we needed another five – not a single – for the record! I was seeing the ball like a breadfruit, too, and I didn't intend throwing my hand away. After all, I had a lot of catching up to do for missed centuries in the past.

Pakistan had another success when Fazal got Everton Weekes at 602 for three – what a score – by which time I was nearing 300 and the excitement began to mount around the ground. You don't have to tell West Indian cricket crowds their records and if there was anyone who did not know what the highest innings in Test cricket was, Roy Lawrence kept reminding them over the radio that it was Len Hutton's 364 against Australia. There was also a great deal of reference to the 337 which Hanif had made in the first Test of that series in Barbados, which was the highest in a West Indian Test, and George Headley's 344 not out against an English touring team back in the 1930s, which was the highest in a first-class match in the West Indies.

When Clyde Walcott came in, he told me that our skipper, Gerry Alexander, was thinking of declaring. Since we were almost 300 ahead, that seemed in order but, although I haven't spoken to him about it, I'm sure Gerry decided to continue once I passed 300.

By that time, the place was humming. Sabina Park is a small ground and, in those days, with spectators hanging onto the light pylons, dangling from trees and with their legs through the double-decked stands at the northern end, it was like a bull-ring. It was then, and only then, that I settled in my mind that I could get that Hutton record – in fact, that I *would* get that record. Clyde kept urging me on: 'Settle down, take it easy. The runs will come and I'll give you as much of the strike as possible.'

The way I approached it was to tell myself that I had just come in to bat, that I didn't have 300 on the board and that, instead, I only needed to score 64 to win the match or to post 1000 for the season. Funnily, even though I had been batting for something like nine hours, I didn't feel tired at all and the depleted Pakistani attack was, by now, in no state to stop the runs flowing.

Suddenly, it seemed, I was on 364. Hutton's record was equalled and the crowd was really in a frenzy. With one needed, Hanif Mohammad, the little batsman who hardly ever bowled, came on. He had had an over before but had bowled it right-handed. Now he informed me – and the umpire – that he was going to bowl left-handed.

'You can bowl with both hands if you like,' I said. His first ball I pushed into the covers, Clyde called for the single and it was there. In a split second, the place was pure bedlam. The crowd streamed across the ground and lifted me in the air and, for a time, I was on cloud nine – almost literally. It is impossible for me to adequately describe my feelings at that moment. Naturally, I was happy. This was not just an ordinary record: it was a Test record. But do you know what I remember? That I felt guilty that I had somehow held up the game and that we were losing time!

In fact, the crowd invasion caused damage to the pitch and the Pakistani captain, Kardar, a hard man at the best of times, complained that it would be unfair to continue until it was repaired. So there was no more play that day which still had about an hour to go. If there had been play without interruption, I'm sure Gerry would have allowed me to add a few more runs before he declared, but what's the difference?

It was only later, much later, as the congratulations came flooding in and people kept coming up and saying that it was one record which would last forever, that what I had achieved began to sink in.

What had started out as a determined effort to score my first Test century after fourteen Tests without one had developed into something really big, as Berkeley Gaskin and Roy Lawrence said it would. In fact, my next two innings in that series, in the fourth Test at Bourda, also produced centuries so that my own 'four-minute barrier' had been well and truly broken.

West Indies v Pakistan, Kingston, 1957–58 (3rd Test)

Pakistan

Hanif Mohammad	c Alexander b Gilchrist	3	b Gilchrist	13
Imtiaz Ahmed†	c Alexander b Gilchrist	122	lbw b Dewdney	0
Saeed Ahmed	c Weekes b Smith	52	c Gilchrist b Gibbs	44
W. Mathias	b Dewdney	77	c Alexander b Atkinson	19
Alimuddin	c Alexander b Atkinson	15	b Gibbs	30
A. H. Kardar*	c Sobers b Atkinson	15	lbw b Dewdney (7)	57
Wazir Mohammad	c Walcott b Dewdney	2	lbw b Atkinson (6)	106
Fazal Mahmood	c Alexander b Atkinson	6	c Alexander b Atkinson	0
Nasim-ul-Ghani	b Atkinson	5	absent hurt	–
Mahmood Hussain	b Atkinson	20	absent hurt	–
Khan Mohammad	not out	3	not out (9)	0
Extras	(LB 5, NB 3)	8	(B 16, LB 3)	19
Total		**328**		**288**

West Indies

C. C. Hunte	run out	260
R. B. Kanhai	c Imtiaz b Fazal	25
G. St A. Sobers	not out	365
E. de C. Weekes	c Hanif b Fazal	39
C. L. Walcott	not out	88
O. G. Smith		
F. C. M. Alexander*†		
L. R. Gibbs		
E. St E. Atkinson	} did not bat	
R. Gilchrist		
D. T. Dewdney		
Extras	(B 2, LB 7, W 4)	13
Total	(3 wickets declared)	**790**

West Indies	O	M	R	W		O	M	R	W
Gilchrist	25	3	106	2		12	3	65	1
Dewdney	26	4	88	2		19.3	2	51	2
Atkinson	21	7	42	5		18	6	36	3
Gibbs	7	0	32	0		21	6	46	2
Smith	18	3	39	1		8	2	20	0
Sobers	5	1	13	0		15	4	41	0
Weekes						3	1	10	0

Pakistan	O	M	R	W
Mahmood Hussain	0.5	0	2	0
Fazal	85.2	20	247	2
Khan	54	5	259	0
Nasim	15	3	39	0
Kardar	37	2	141	0
Wallis	4	0	20	0
Alimuddin	4	0	34	0
Hanif	2	0	11	0
Saeed	6	0	24	0

Gary Sobers' Most Memorable Matches

Sunday Advocate, Barbados, 2 March 1958: 'Pandemonium broke out here this afternoon at Sabina Park on the fourth day of the third Test match ... after 21-year-old Barbadian Garfield Sobers had beaten Sir Leonard Hutton's Test record score of 364.

'The unprecedented display of enthusiastic, but bad behaviour by a section of the record crowd of 20,000 that watched the day's play brought an abrupt ending 55 minutes before the scheduled close in an atmosphere of wild scenes and confusion that marred the glamour, brilliance and history-making achievement of the gifted left-hander to whom the day completely belonged and whose name will not only adorn the record book for a very long time but also is likely to become a legend in West Indies cricket.

'For 608 minutes, Sobers dominated the depleted Pakistan attack and, in his chanceless innings of 365, during which he had hit 37 fours, he had thrilled this animated crowd.'

8 In the Breach with Worrell

West Indies v England, Bridgetown, 1960

I wouldn't describe Kensington Oval in Bridgetown as one of the world's great cricket grounds. It is somewhat small, lacks facilities you find in Australia, England and, nowadays, India and doesn't have the beauty of the mountains in the distance of which Queen's Park Oval in Trinidad and Sabina Park in Jamaica can boast. Yet, to me, Kensington has always been home, where I played my first big cricket. It may lack for other things but, in my time, you could be sure that the head groundsman, little Jimmy Bowen, would turn out a magnificent pitch and that the spectators would be there to appreciate the finer points of the game.

For much of my early career, I played most of my first-class and Test cricket away from Kensington. Between my debut Test in 1954 and the England tour of the West Indies in 1960, I'd had only two Tests at Kensington – in 1955 against Australia and in 1958 against Pakistan – and about half-a-dozen first-class matches. Sure, I had played club cricket whenever I returned but, what with a contract in the Lancashire League and tours to New Zealand in 1956, England in 1957 and India, Sri Lanka and Pakistan in 1958–59, I hadn't seen Kensington for a long time when Peter May's men arrived in Barbados for the first leg of their tour just before Christmas, 1959.

By then, of course, I had been getting plenty of runs, including the record 365 not out against Pakistan, and I knew Barbados people in general and my friends in particular were looking forward to some big things against the Englishmen.

49

In fact, they told me so in no uncertain terms! Their attitude was that it's all very well to get runs against the Pakistanis and the Indians but you haven't shown your mettle until you get them against England and Australia.

So I had a lot to live up to and, fortunately, I was able to keep everyone happy with a century in the island match and a double – 224 to be exact – in the Test, my first three-figure innings in a Test at Kensington. In each one, I shared a long partnership with a batting artist: in the Barbados match with Seymour Nurse, who was at the start of his international career, and in the Test with Frank Worrell, who was coming to the end of his.

The innings were played within a week of each other and were complete contrasts, in respect both of my own batting and the partnerships. In the island match – or 'colony match' as it was called in those days before Barbados' independence – everything was right for batting. The pitch was a typical Kensington beauty, hard and true with even bounce. The English team, in the West Indies for less than two weeks straight from winter at home, were still feeling their way and Everton Weekes won the toss and we batted in warm, bright sunshine. You *had* to make a few in those conditions although, with Trueman, Statham and Illingworth in the attack, it would be stupid to minimize the quality of the opposition.

As it turned out, Seymour batted magnificently for 213, I made 154 and we put on 306 for the third wicket at better than a run a minute. Barbados piled up 533 for five before Everton declared. Then, with Charlie Griffith in his first big match giving an early warning to English batsmen of what was to follow in the years ahead, we made them follow on and finally won in a desperate and amazing finish by ten wickets, as Cammie Smith and Conrad Hunte belted 58 runs off just over six overs. This was a race against the clock and the weather, since it was actually drizzling when the winning stroke was made.

Naturally, I've had to look into *Wisden* for the statistics and it says there I hit a six and 21 fours. I can't remember the fours but I certainly can recall the six, since it was off my old adversary, Freddie Trueman, and it was a real beauty. I see he's talked a lot in his own *Memorable Matches* about a particular ball with which he bowled me in the Edgbaston Test in 1963, so I'm sure he won't mind me relating that shot.

We were well set when Fred was given the second new ball. He dropped one short and by what happened immediately afterwards I knew it must have been a good bouncer – except that I had hit it, off the back foot, on top of the Kensington Stand at square leg! It wasn't a hook, more a flick and it came off the meat of the bat, one of those shots you play by instinct. I can still 'feel' that shot now . . . and see Fred's reaction. He came down the pitch, mouth open, with that look of astonishment of his. 'Good shot, Sunshine,' he said. 'But that was a bloody good 'un. It didn't deserve to be hit like that.'

Things were a little different a week later in the Test. This time we were the ones who were kept in the hot sun after losing the toss and England batted something like two-and-a-half days for 482. By the end of the third day, we were three wickets down, only just over 100 on the board and, with three days remaining, in some trouble.

When Conrad Hunte was third man out with about half an hour to go, Frank Worrell came in and straight away came up to me. 'We're in trouble here,' he said, 'so we've got to put our heads down and bat our way out of it because there's not much to follow.' In fact, Basil Butcher was the one recognized batsman to come with Gerry Alexander, Wes Hall, Reg Scarlett, Chester Watson and Sonny Ramadhin after that.

Any thoughts I had of playing my shots as I had done in the Barbados match had to be dispelled and Frank never let me forget it. 'Keep your head down,' he would keep on saying, 'we're not out of it yet!' Even when I passed 100, and 150, and 200. He could see what might have happened if we got out, for England were safe with their first innings total.

We eventually added 399 and, by the time Fred went

around the wicket and beat me on the forward stroke to hit the off-stump on the final morning, I had 226 against my name in the book, having batted something like ten-and-three-quarter hours for them. The West Indies were in the lead and the potential trouble of three days earlier seemed a long way off. I don't mind admitting that, although I was only twenty-three and fit as I could be, I was dog-tired. I was also pleased as punch for it had been quite a week for me on the ground I knew as home.

If I was tired, Frank was near to complete collapse. He was now thirty-five years of age and had played no Test cricket – in fact, very little first-class cricket – since 1957. Instead, he had been studying at Manchester University. That he could bat as steadfastly as he did in his first Test for so long was a wonder in itself, but it caused a lot of controversy and comment at the end.

On the final day the crowd, seeing the match petering out, wanted Gerry Alexander to declare early and give Wes Hall and Chester Watson a go at the England batsmen. It really didn't make any difference one way or the other but eventually Gerry did give instructions that he wanted to declare and even signalled Frank from the pavilion to get on with it. When he didn't, Gerry declared with Frank at 197 not out, three short of a double century.

Some of the crowd booed Frank and there was a lot of silly talk that he batted as he did because he wanted to be captain or because he didn't like the Barbados crowd. It was all nonsense to those of us who knew Frank. The fact of the matter was that he was physically and mentally exhausted, all in, 'out to the baller'. I remember sitting near him in the dressing room during intervals in our partnership saying how hard it was to keep going, but keep going he must. His state of mind was hardly surprising after more than eleven hours in the middle!

The way the crowd reacted to his batting on the final day was unjust to such a great player, now in middle age, who had instigated our fight back and who had influenced me to

West Indies v England, Bridgetown, 1959–60 (1st Test)

England

G. Pullar	run out	65	not out		46
M. C. Cowdrey	c Sobers b Watson	30	not out		16
K. F. Barrington	c Alexander b Ramadhin	128			
P. B. H. May*	c Alexander b Hall	1			
M. J. K. Smith	c Alexander b Scarlett	39			
E. R. Dexter	not out	136			
R. Illingworth	b Ramadhin	5			
R. Swetman†	c Alexander b Worrell	45			
F. S. Trueman	c Alexander b Ramadhin	3			
D. A. Allen	lbw b Watson	10			
A. E. Moss	b Watson	4			
Extras	(B 4, LB 6, NB 6)	16	(B 7, LB 1, W 1)		9
Total		**482**	(0 wickets)		**71**

West Indies

C. C. Hunte	c Swetman b Barrington	42
E. D. A. St J. McMorris	run out	0
R. B. Kanhai	b Trueman	40
G. St A. Sobers	b Trueman	226
F. M. M. Worrell	not out	197
B. F. Butcher	c Trueman b Dexter	13
W. W. Hall	lbw b Trueman	14
F. C. M. Alexander*†	c Smith b Trueman	3
R. G. Scarlett	lbw b Dexter	7
C. D. Watson	} did not bat	
S. Ramadhin		
Extras	B 8, LB 7, W 1, NB 5)	21
Total	(8 wickets declared)	**563**

West Indies	O	M	R	W	O	M	R	W
Hall	40	9	98	1	6	2	9	0
Watson	32.4	6	121	3	8	1	19	0
Worrell	15	2	39	1				
Ramadhin	54	22	109	3	7	2	11	0
Scarlett	26	9	46	1	10	4	12	0
Sobers	21	3	53	0				
Hunte					7	2	9	0
Kanhai					4	3	2	0

England	O	M	R	W
Trueman	47	15	93	4
Moss	47	14	116	0
Dexter	37.4	11	85	2
Illingworth	47	9	106	0
Allen	43	12	82	0
Barrington	18	3	60	

bat the way I did. It's a pity the spectators can't sometimes appreciate what goes on behind the scenes.

English writer E. W. Swanton: 'These two great West Indies batsmen played wonderfully well, though in a mood of strong restraint, which was only relaxed quite late in the day. With an hour to go the skies clouded, the rain came and England were reprieved. Sobers had just reached his hundred with Worrell only nine short.

'Sobers had taken five hours 20 minutes over it and it came rather as a surprise to recall that this was his first century either against England or Australia, though he has taken three apiece from the Indians and Pakistanis.

'One remembers him so well, coming in with the strange gangling walk as a lad of seventeen against England at Kingston six years ago. He was a player of unmistakeable class then: now he is the finished article, an experienced, balanced, fully organized cricketer who should have a glittering part to play in the Test cricket of the next decade.'

(Reproduced from *West Indies Revisited*, 1960.)

9 The Incredible Tie

West Indies v Australia, Brisbane, 1960–61

Australia has occupied a prominent place in my life. I have played a lot of my cricket there, made hundreds of friends, taken an Australian girl as my wife, and lived and worked in Melbourne, together with my family, for several years.

The happy relationship started with my first tour to Australia in 1960–61 – undoubtedly, from every possible point of view, the best I have ever been on. On the field, two evenly matched attacking teams each led by an inspiring captain contested an incredible series which produced the one and only tied result in Test cricket history, included two other nail-biting finishes and was only decided in Australia's favour on the final day. There were several stirring individual performances by some of the greats of the modern era.

But it was more than just the cricket which made that trip so unforgettable. The players from the two sides got on like life-long friends and mixed freely and easily, while the Australian people were warm and spontaneous in their hospitality. It was, in every respect, an experience which had a tremendous effect on my cricket and my life generally.

The memories of that tour come flooding back whenever those of us who took part in it start talking about old times and there is certainly one innings and one match which I'll always cherish – the first Test, the incredible tie, in which I made 132 in our first innings. Like all the teams in the past, we started our tour in Perth where we got the feel of Australian pitches and the high, all-round standard of their cricket. We lost to Western Australia and drew against a combined

55

Australian XI, containing some of those certain to play in their Test team. We then headed east and, by the time the first Test came around, had played all the states and had given such an inconsistent performance that we weren't rated very highly by the press.

By then, yours truly was in a bad patch with the bat and there was a lot of talk about my technique in Australian conditions and my ability against leg-spin. I'd been in pretty good form in Perth with a century against Western Australia and 70-odd against the Combined team but, after that, the runs dried up. It wasn't the first time it had happened and I was not particularly worried. But the press made a song and dance about it, especially when I was bowled by the first ball I faced from Richie Benaud in the match against the powerful New South Wales team.

With the first Test coming up, the papers were writing us off because of our heavy defeat by an innings and were already putting Richie down as my 'bogey man'. The fact is that I got a good ball, didn't play it too well and it came between bat and pad to hit the off-stump. It certainly wasn't the end of the world but I suppose I was looking a little glum when our skipper Frank Worrell brought the great Sir Donald Bradman into the dressing room at the Sydney Cricket Ground to introduce him to the boys. Truth was I was concentrating on cricket and, possibly, my own failure and hadn't noticed Sir Don there until I felt someone put his hand on my head playfully and say: 'Don' you worry, son, you'll get them at the right time.'

As far as I was concerned, the right time would have to be the first Test, less than two weeks off in Brisbane. When we got to the Gabba ground on the morning of the match, Sir Don was again there, in his capacity as Australian selector, and as he strolled by, he turned to me to say: 'I hope you're not going to disappoint me this time.' I didn't have any intention of disappointing Sir Don, myself or the West Indies team for, I must admit, I was a little peeved at my lack of runs since I hadn't passed 30 since Perth.

I had to go in somewhat earlier than I'd hoped since Alan Davidson carried away Cammie Smith and Conrad Hunte fairly quickly, then added Rohan Kanhai before we had 50 on the board. So, you might say, the stage was set for the performance which Sir Donald had commanded.

It was one of those days when you know, from the first ball, that you're at your best and I made up my mind I wouldn't be wasting this kind of form. The pitch was a beauty and I was seeing the ball as big as a breadfruit. In no time, it seemed, I reached 50 and I couldn't remember having played better.

Davidson and Ian Meckiff shared the new ball and then Ken Mackay bowled a few gentle swingers first change. But everyone knew the real confrontation would be when Richie brought himself on. It wasn't long. In his first over, I went back and he thought he was through me, throwing his hands in the air.

Not this time! I was well set and hit it back past him in a flash for four. The fact was that Richie never really bowled a big googly, especially on a good pitch which this was. He was a brilliant leg-spinner and had a tremendous top-spinner or 'flipper' as the Aussies called it. But, that day, I got my own back for the first ball he'd given me in the New South Wales match. By the time I was caught off, of all things, a full toss from Meckiff, I'd scored 132 in under three hours with 21 fours. It was a 'sweet hand' as we used to say in the Bayland in the old days and when I got back to the pavilion, one of the first to come up to me was The Don. 'Well, you didn't disappoint me,' he said.

Of course, I couldn't just bat like that without someone holding out at the other end and Frank Worrell, cool-headed and steady, used all of his experience to make sure there was no breakthrough. In the end we made over 450.

It was to be the beginning of an incredible cricket match. Australia, with Norman O'Neill hitting 181, topped 500. Usually, such first innings totals spell a certain draw in Test cricket. Somehow another 20 wickets were still to fall and, as everyone with even an inkling of cricket knowledge will know, the match ended off the last but one ball with scores exactly equal, the first tie in Test cricket.

Perhaps a computer can calculate the odds on all 40 wickets falling in a cricket match of five days' duration in which almost 1500 runs are scored, ending in a tie with a single ball remaining. But they are long odds. Of course, it was a fluke, but not a complete fluke. At no stage did we feel that the match was out of our grasp or that a draw was inevitable. Throughout, Frank kept pressing on, convincing us that we would win. Richie, I believe, had the same attitude. They were two truly great captains, fine players both, excellent readers of the game and able to inspire their men.

What can I say about the final frenzied over that hasn't been said before? When it started, six runs were needed by Australia to win; we required three wickets. They got five and we got our wickets amidst a lot of frantic excitement, including the final run out of Meckiff by Joe Solomon with his direct hit from square-leg.

When that happened, there were a lot of us who didn't know quite what the result was. I remember Rohan Kanhai being so excited that we'd won. Frank Worrell, who never seemed flustered in spite of all the drama, knew. 'Imagine, a tie!' he said, cool as a cucumber, when we were sprinting off the field.

No one who was involved in it will ever forget that match and especially that final over. Wes Hall, with that elongated, explosive run-in of his, bowled it. His personality, I feel, helped make the finish even more thrilling than it would have been had, say, a spinner been bowling.

Wes was all action and in the historic film of that final over, which I've seen several times since, he is the one who creates the excitement bounding in, following through, throwing his hands in the air and even, once, managing to run to square-leg and drop a skier off Wally Grout!

Australia v West Indies, Brisbane, 1960–61 (1st Test)

West Indies

C. C. Hunte	c Benaud b Davidson	24	c Simpson b Mackay	39
C. W. Smith	c Grout b Davidson	7	c O'Neill b Davidson	6
R. B. Kanhai	c Grout b Davidson	15	c Grout b Davidson	54
G. St A. Sobers	c Kline b Meckiff	132	b Davidson	14
F. M. M. Worrell*	c Grout b Davidson	65	c Grout b Davidson	65
J. S. Solomon	hit wkt b Simpson	65	lbw b Simpson	47
P. D. Lashley	c Grout b Kline	19	b Davidson	0
F. C. M. Alexander†	c Davidson b Kline	60	b Benaud	5
S. Ramadhin	c Harvey b Davidson	12	c Harvey b Simpson	6
W. W. Hall	st Grout b Kline	50	b Davidson	18
A. L. Valentine	not out	0	not out	7
Extras	(LB 3, W 1)	4	(B 14, LB 7, W 2)	23
Total		**453**		**284**

Australia

C. C. McDonald	c Hunte b Sobers	57	b Worrell	16
R. B. Simpson	b Ramadhin	92	c sub (L. R. Gibbs) b Hall	0
R. N. Harvey	b Valentine	15	c Sobers b Hall	5
N. C. O'Neill	c Valentine b Hall	181	c Alexander b Hall	26
L. E. Favell	run out	45	c Solomon b Hall	7
K. D. Mackay	b Sobers	35	b Ramadhin	28
A. K. Davidson	c Alexander b Hall	44	run out	80
R. Benaud*	lbw b Hall	10	c Alexander b Hall	52
A. T. W. Grout†	lbw b Hall	4	run out	2
I. Meckiff	run out	4	run out	2
L. F. Kline	not out	3	not out	0
Extras	(B 2, LB 8, W 1, NB 4)	15	(B 2, LB 9, NB 3)	14
Total		**505**		**232**

Australia	O	M	R	W		O	M	R	W
Davidson	30	2	135	5		24.6	4	87	6
Meckiff	18	0	129	1		4	1	19	0
Mackay	3	0	15	0		21	7	52	1
Benaud	24	3	93	0		31	6	69	1
Simpson	8	0	25	1		7	2	18	2
Kline	17.6	6	52	3		4	0	14	0
O'Neill						1	0	2	0

West Indies	O	M	R	W		O	M	R	W
Hall	29.3	1	140	4		17.7	3	63	5
Worrell	30	0	93	0		16	3	41	1
Sobers	32	0	115	2		8	0	30	0
Valentine	24	6	82	1		10	4	27	0
Ramadhin	15	1	60	1		17	3	57	1

Australian broadcaster and writer A. G. 'Johnnie' Moyes: 'Sobers and Worrell were now together and they provided some of the loveliest batting seen on Australian playing fields for many years. Sobers, who had had a lean patch, ran into his finest form at the critical time, his driving, cutting and on-side play so masterly that one ran out of superlatives in describing his strokes.

'. . .The pair ran to their 150 partnership in only 134 minutes, so complete was their mastery of the bowling and then, 18 minutes later, Sobers was out, caught off a somewhat careless-looking stroke to a full toss just outside his pads. His 132 was made in 174 minutes and he hit 21 fours in an innings which ranks with the most outstanding seen in Australia since the halcyon days of Bradman and McCabe.

'It had everything needed to make it ever memorable: glorious strokes, abundant power, beauty in execution, calm assurance and a brilliance that set the field alight and sent a warm glow through all those who were spectators.'

(Reproduced from *With the West Indies in Australia, 1960–61: A Critical Story of the Tour.*)

10 The Day Davo's Bouncer Went West

South Australia v New South Wales, Adelaide, 1961

Cricket has become so internationalized that the player of today can turn out for a county team in England, a state team in Australia and, if he is prepared to accept the consequences, a provincial team in South Africa all in the same year. It was a process which started in the 1960s and which allowed me to get a taste of Sheffield Shield cricket and English county cricket in addition to our own domestic cricket in the West Indies.

Things may have changed, but I would rate Sheffield Shield cricket – as it was when I played three seasons for South Australia between 1961 and 1965 – as the strongest and most competitive of the three. The Shell Shield in the West Indies and, before that, the quadrangular tournament, were certainly not far behind, with English county cricket not really comparable. Not, at least, from my own county experiences and those were with Nottinghamshire in the 1970s.

Shield cricket in both Australia and the West Indies was contested between only five teams (six nowadays) which meant that there was a high concentration of the best players in those teams. The English county championship is spread over seventeen teams, so the top players are more widely spread.

My three seasons with South Australia were most enjoyable and rewarding and served to strengthen my feeling for Australia following the West Indies tour of 1960–61. In the second and third seasons I did the 'double' of 1000 runs and 50 wickets in all first-class matches and eventually was on the

61

team which won the Shield for South Australia for the first time in ten seasons.

No overseas player had participated in Australian domestic cricket prior to 1961–62 but the popularity of the West Indies team on our tour the previous season was enough to break the barrier. Wes Hall, who went to Queensland, Rohan Kanhai, who went to Western Australia, and myself were invited back and, even though there was the inevitable criticism from those who felt Australian home cricket should be limited to Australians, it was mild and we found ourselves generally well-accepted by the public. It is interesting to note that, since then, a host of overseas players have played state cricket. Colin Milburn, Tom Graveney, Rusi Surti, Barry Richards, Jack Simmons, Andy Roberts, Viv Richards, Joel Garner and so on.

Our first season proved to be a highly successful one, with big crowds at all the matches and tremendous interest, comparable to what I experienced back home in the West Indies for the inter-island games. There was no distraction of a Test series at the time, and the Sheffield Shield held full attention. Somehow, however, I just couldn't get going. While Rohan took a brilliant century off us in his very first match and Wes was scattering wickets all over the place for Queensland, I found wickets and runs hard to come by.

As it was, I couldn't finish the season since I had to get back to the West Indies by mid-February for the Test series against India and, by the time my last match came around, my figures were very moderate. I felt I had to do something, but the match was against New South Wales, the perennial champions who fielded one of the strongest teams in the world outside of Test cricket and who had swept through the season to date unbeaten. They defeated us comfortably in our first match in Sydney and you could understand why they were doing as well as they were with just a glance at their team: Richie Benaud was captain, Bobby Simpson, Ian Craig, Neil Harvey, Norman O'Neill, Brian Booth, Graeme Thomas,

Alan Davidson, Johnnie Martin and Frank Martin, Test players all, with Doug Ford, their very fine wicket-keeper.

We batted first in the second match at Adelaide and when we were out for 190 (G. Sobers caught behind off Davidson for 2) we looked down and out again. Still, we kept them to a lead of around 50 so we were not out of contention and, finally and at the most opportune moment, I came good with a vengeance in the second innings. I made 251, which enabled us to declare about 400 ahead and then I took six wickets as we bowled them out to inflict on them their only defeat of the season. It seems as if I'd stored up all my form for that one match and I was more than pleased that I had at least gone some way to living up to the expectations of the South Australian Cricket Association and the Coca-Cola company which had brought me out there.

It's a long time ago and, apart from the circumstances of the match, I don't remember too many details. But one shot will always remain with me and I hear they still talk about it at the Adelaide Oval. That ground is a peculiar shape with short side boundaries and extremely long straight ones. I've known batsmen to run five on straight hits or strokes down to fine leg and third man, which is no wonder since they measure something like 110 yards.

In that innings, I had made something like 150 when Alan Davidson, that great left-arm fast bowler who had got me cheaply twice in three innings that season, took the second new ball. The very first delivery was a beamer that came straight at my head and all I could do was take reflex action to protect myself. The ball flew off the back of the bat and went through the slips for four. In a flash, Alan was down to me apologizing for the delivery but, accidental or not, it did rile me.

A couple of overs later, he banged one in short, a bouncer. By then, I was seeing everything very early and I got into position and slapped it, with a flat bat, from outside the off-stump. It must have hit the dead-centre of that Slazenger bat and, with the hardness of the new ball, it just went, and went, and finally landed on the scoreboard. It was a carry of fully 150 yards and I couldn't believe it myself. I'd never hit a ball that far before and never have done since. Whenever I go back to the Adelaide Oval I glance up at the distance between the pitch and that scoreboard and still wonder if I was dreaming. Les Favell, who was our skipper in those days, keeps assuring me it *did* happen.

It's the kind of singular incident in sport that builds up into a legend – like Henry Cooper's left cross which floored Muhammad Ali or Geoff Hurst's goal which won the World Cup for England. I'll always cherish that stroke, more especially since Davo's beamer that day might not have been accidental after all. Like all fast bowlers, he had a fiery temper on the field and, when I got back to Adelaide the following season, Col Egar, who was umpiring that match, reminded me of the beamer. 'You know, Gary, I don't believe that it slipped at all. When he passed me as he walked back he said, "I'll show him a thing or two!" '

Well, all's fair in love and Sheffield Shield cricket!

Australian writer Ray Robinson: 'Sobers electrified the crowd with a backfoot drive off Davidson for the longest six hit in Australia since the war. Surviving difficult slip chances at 105 and 156, he passed 200 in 326 minutes, dealing mercilessly with every bowler except Benaud whose five for 121 in 35 overs contained some of the finest bowling of his career.

'When Gary cracked a four off one Davidson bouncer, former Test captain Victor Richardson said: "You have to be here to believe what's happening. Sobers' strokes possess rhythm and perfection." '

(Reproduced from the *Barbados Advocate*, 13 February 1962.)

South Australia v New South Wales, Adelaide, 1961–62

South Australia

L. Favell*	c Craig b Davidson	28	c O'Neill b Davidson	8
J. Lill	c Martin b Misson	8	b Benaud	51
G. St A. Sobers	c Ford b Davidson	2	b Davidson	251
I. McLachlan	c Ford b Davidson	7	b Martin	5
N. Dansie	c Simpson b Davidson	40	b Benaud	71
R. Lloyd	c Ford b Davidson	1	c Booth b Benaud	35
N. Hawke	c Thomas b Misson	0	not out	6
B. Jarman†	c Benaud b Misson	15	c Martin b Benaud	12
R. Sellers	c Craig b Booth	33	c Martin b Benaud	9
D. Sincock	not out	52		
G. Brooks	b Benaud	1		
Extras	(LB 1, NB 2)	3	(B4, LB 5, W 1, NB 1)	11
Total		**190**		**459**

New South Wales

R. Simpson	c Jarman b Brooks	19	st Jarman b Sobers	1
I. Craig	lbw b Sobers	32	c Jarman b Sobers	56
N. O'Neill	c Brooks b Sincock	1	c Brooks b Sobers	43
B. Booth	lbw b Brooks	9	st Jarman b Sincock	28
N. Harvey	st Jarman b Sincock	39	b Sobers	22
G. Thomas	c Lill b Sobers	6	c Favell b Sincock	28
A. Davidson	c Jarman b Sobers	0	c Favell b Sincock	9
R Benaud*	c Jarman b Brooks	19	not out	38
J. Martin	c Jarman b Hawke	63	Sobers	9
M. Misson	not out	51	c Jarman b Sobers	4
D. Ford†	c Jarman b Hawke	6	lbw b Hawke	27
Extras	(LB 4)	4	(B 2, LB 1, W 1, NB 1)	5
Total		**249**		**270**

New South Wales	O	M	R	W	O	M	R	W
Davidson	17	5	40	5	25	0	99	2
Misson	12	2	38	3	9	1	39	0
Simpson	13	0	52	0	11	3	43	0
Martin	5	0	37	0	18	0	121	1
Booth	8	2	12	1				
Benaud	6.6	0	8	1	34.3	6	121	5
O'Neill					5	0	25	0

South Australia	O	M	R	W	O	M	R	W
Brooks	18	0	53	3	11	1	52	0
Hawke	11.4	2	41	2	7.4	2	20	1
Sincock	17	0	78	2	18	2	96	3
Sobers	14	1	51	3	23	3	72	6
Sellers	3	0	22	0	4	0	17	0
Dansie					3	0	8	0

11 The Slip With No Sleep
West Indies v India, Port-of-Spain, 1962

You hear a lot these days about how much the modern cricketer travels and there is certainly much to keep him occupied. On the international schedule it is difficult to remember who is playing who, where and when. Yet I wonder if anyone can match my own experience of jet-age cricket back in February 1962.

After our rousing series in Australia in 1960–61, I accepted the invitation to play for South Australia. The trouble was that the end of the Australian season overlapped with the first Test of the home series against India, which meant missing a Shield match or two.

In my case, I was anxious to squeeze in South Australia's game against the great New South Wales team of the time at Adelaide even if it did mean a mad scramble to get back to Port-of-Spain, the venue for the first Test against India. The West Indies Board had already asked us if we were available. We said we were and Wes and Rohan had gone off the week before.

As far as I was concerned, it meant some pretty deft work at airports, changing planes and making the right connections. The Adelaide match ended on 13 February; the Test started on 16 February. Anyone who knows where Adelaide is on the map in relation to Port-of-Spain will appreciate the problem. The way I saw it, I could leave Australia on the 14th, get into New York on the 15th and make a same-day connection to Trinidad. I might be tired when I got there, but at least I would get there.

The best laid plans of mice and men, as they say! I certainly left Australia with a bang. I'd had a disappointing season but now everything came good, with 251 in South Australia's second innings against an attack including Alan Davidson, Richie Benaud, Frank Misson and Johnnie Martin, all Australian Test players. And then I took six for 72 to inflict the only defeat the mighty NSW suffered all season.

There was no time for celebrating, however. It was straight to the Adelaide airport, hopping onto Trans-Australia Airlines for Sydney and then the long haul across the Pacific and across America to New York. In those days, the plane kept putting down to refuel on the way at Fiji, Honolulu, San Francisco. By the time it reached New York, it seemed as if we'd been flying for weeks.

Still, I was on schedule. Early morning, 15 February. Now a flight down to Trinidad, six hours at the most, in good time for the Test. But what flight? At the time, the Caribbean airline, BWIA, didn't fly into New York so I had to depend on BOAC, as it then was, or Pan-American. Sorry, said BOAC, our next flight is in two days' time. Pan-Am couldn't oblige either.

By now I was frantic for I didn't want to miss that Test and let down our skipper, Frank Worrell. As you may be aware, New York is not exactly a city where a cricket Test match means much. In Barbados or Kingston, or even in London or Sydney, I might have been able to inspire a bit of action from some cricket fan with an airline. Not here, Buster!

In the end, someone suggested the Brazilian airline, Varig, which was in transit at Trinidad airport. So I tried it. Bingo! Yes, they had a flight leaving at one in the morning and I could get on it. By this time, two-and-a-half days in the field at Adelaide, another day-and-a-half in a plane and all the hurrying and scurrying around New York Airport were beginning to have their effect and a few brandies came in handy.

Perhaps the brandies fired my imagination but I swear to you that when we were about to take off, I looked out of the window and there was one of the engines spewing flames. It did put a scare into me although no one else seemed very bothered. We took off and had a wonderful flight down. I can't remember exactly what time we arrived, but when I joined the team that morning, there was a lot of good-natured ribbing at my expense – although I got the impression that they were all happy to see me.

As fate would have it, India won the toss and batted. Standing on a cricket field for a few hours after all my travelling was the last thing I wanted at that stage, yet we couldn't very well ask for a sub, could we?

So out we went, yours truly stationed, as usual, at second slip. Later, friends in Barbados who were listening to the broadcast told me this almost caused Sir Learie Constantine, broadcasting on the match, to have apoplexy. He had once travelled overnight to get to India for a match, he said. He had been put in the slips and had promptly dropped two catches – a rare occurrence in ordinary circumstances. I had travelled even further and had only had time to pull on my trousers. No, slips were definitely no place for me.

Apparently, it was a subject which occupied his attention for some time – until, after about an hour, Nari Contractor snicked one off Wes and I caught it low down at second slip. Sir Learie's response, apparently, was that these things do happen. Not long after there was another snick, this time from Polly Umrigar off Chester Watson, and the catch stuck again. 'This boy's impossible,' was Sir Learie's final comment.

I also had a few overs that day and picked up a couple of wickets but, if the truth be known, I *was* flat out at the end of it and slept long and sound that night. After that, I did a lot of international travelling by jetliners but I always made sure to give myself enough time between assignments. From one match in Australia to another in Trinidad with only *two* days in between is not to be recommended to anyone!

West Indian cricket writer and commentator Tony Cozier: 'Not the least staggering feature of the day was the appearance of Sobers who, having completed his one-man demolition of New South Wales for South Australia on one side of the globe just three days ago, only ended a tortuous journey back to the Caribbean in the early hours of the morning.

'Yet, there he was on the field, identified with the two other Australian state players, Hall and Kanhai, by handkerchiefs tied nattily around their necks, ready to pounce on anything that came his way. With the ball moving around, it was inevitable that something would happen and soon, defying medical theory about 'jet-lag', he was casually collecting slip catches off Contractor and Umrigar.'

(From the *Barbados Daily News*, 17 February 1962.)

West Indies v India, Port-of-Spain, 1961–62 (1st Test)

India

Batsman	First innings		Second innings	
N. J. Contractor*	c Sobers b Hall	10	b Hall	6
V. L. Mehra	c Hendriks b Hall	0	b Stayers	8
V. L. Manjrekar	b Stayers	19	hit wkt b Hall	0
D. N. Sardesai	c Solomon b Stayers	16	c Smith b Hall	2
P. R. Umrigar	c Sobers b Watson	2	c sub (W. V. Rodriguez) b Sobers	23
C. G. Borde	c Gibbs b Stayers	16	b Sobers	27
S. A. Durani	c and b Sobers	56	c Worrell b Sobers	7
R. F. Surti	st Smith b Sobers	57	c sub (W. V. Rodriguez) b Sobers	0
R. G. Nadkarni	run out	2	not out	12
F. M. Engineer†	c (sub W. V. Rodriguez) b Gibbs	3	c and b Gibbs	2
R. B. Desai	not out	4	c Kanhai b Gibbs	2
Extras	(B 11, LB 5, NB 2)	18	(LB 4, W 1, NB 4)	9
Total		**203**		**98**

West Indies

Batsman	First innings		Second innings	
C. C. Hunte	c and b Durani	58	not out	10
C. W. Smith	c Umrigar b Desai	12	not out	4
R. B. Kanhai	c and b Borde	24		
G. St A. Sobers	b Umrigar	40		
F. M. M. Worrell*	c Surti b Durani	0		
J. S. Solomon	c Engineer b Desai	43		
S. C. Stayers	c Borde b Durani	4		
J. L. Hendriks†	c Durani b Borde	64		
L. R. Gibbs	c Durani b Umrigar	0		
W. W. Hall	not out	37		
C. D. Watson	c Contractor b Durani	0		
Extras	(B 4, LB 3)	7	(NB 1)	1
Total		**289**	(0 wickets)	**15**

West Indies	O	M	R	W	O	M	R	W
Hall	20	6	38	2	8	3	11	3
Watson	12	4	20	1	4	2	6	0
Stayers	18	1	65	3	8	4	20	1
Gibbs	14	4	34	1	7.5	1	16	2
Sobers	9.3	1	28	2	15	7	22	4
Worrell					8	2	14	0

India	O	M	R	W	O	M	R	W
Desai	13	3	46	2	1	0	5	0
Umrigar	35	8	77	2				
Durani	35.2	9	82	4				
Borde	25	4	65	2				
Nadkarni	3	2	1	0				
Surti	2	0	11	0	0.4	0	9	0

12 The Septic Tonk
West Indies v England, Leeds, 1963

Someone once asked me on a radio interview how I'd managed to keep going without missing a single Test match between 1955 and 1973. It was a question I had never really considered and all I can say with hindsight is that someone up there was looking after me. I certainly didn't train harder than anyone else, but I never ducked out of matches either – no matter how unimportant they might have appeared. I never wore a thigh pad, far less a helmet, and faced a few quick bowlers in my time. I can't even remember pulling a muscle.

There was one occasion, however, when I very nearly did have to withdraw from the Test team. In the end, I didn't and, as so often happens in such cases, I produced one of my best all-round performances. The Test in question was the fourth of that magnificent 1963 series against England at Leeds. We went into the match all square. We won the first Test at Old Trafford, there was a fantastic draw in the second Test, when Colin Cowdrey came in with his broken hand in a sling to stay at the non-striker's end for the last two balls, and then England won at Edgbaston.

So the Leeds Test was a key match. However, a few days before it a whitlow on one of the fingers of my right hand came off and the finger turned septic. Anyone who has gone through that type of agony will know how I was feeling. It throbbed something terrible and yet I found myself included in the side for the match against Middlesex at Lord's which preceded the Test. Needless to say, I wasn't very pleased and simply could do no more than bowl a few overs on the opening day. I couldn't bat and tried all sorts of remedies without success. By the time we reached Leeds, nothing had worked and the pain was still so unbearable that I had to have my arm in a sling to prevent the throbbing.

It was one match I didn't want to miss; I hated missing *any* cricket and this was the match which would probably decide the series. More specifically, Rohan Kanhai and myself were being taunted that we had yet to make a Test century in England, after two tours. The critics kept saying that any batsman worth his salt had to prove himself in English conditions. It was all right to pile up big scores in the hot countries on hard pitches but you couldn't prove your worth until you made runs on an English green top against the moving ball. While I had made runs in both county and league matches, it was not the same as getting them in a Test and I was desperately keen to silence the critics. But how could I?

I had a try-out in the nets and that certainly didn't give me any confidence and there was no way that I wanted to be in the team and then find, as I did in the Middlesex match, that I had to go into the scorebook as 'absent hurt' or 'retired hurt'. Critical situations require critical action and the doctor decided to lance the finger on the morning before the match to release the infection. But this meant it would still be extremely sore and would have to be plastered. The doc's advice was not to play, but he left the decision up to me. I left my decision up to the skipper, Frank Worrell.

When he said: 'You've got to play,' that's all I wanted to hear. Frank had, by this time, established himself almost as a god to all of us and once he gave the go-ahead, I knew it would be accepted by the team as a whole.

Naturally, I hoped we would field first so I could spend a few hours without having to put the finger to the test. No such luck. Frank won the toss, we batted and by lunch I was gingerly pulling on my glove over my plastered finger and walking out, a little apprehensively I must admit, to join Rohan Kanhai.

So here we were together, both of us anxious to prove ourselves with a Test century in England at last, and with the West Indies in some trouble. Fortunately for me, the finger was not as bad as I had feared. Yes, there was pain when it jarred against the bat handle, especially when Freddie Trueman was in operation, but it was nothing to upset my concentration and we carried on our partnership until after tea with over 200 on the board, both of us well in sight of that elusive century.

Rohan didn't get his. He had made 92 when Tony Lock was brought into the attack and produced one to sneak under the bat and bowl him. Rohan had to wait until the last Test of the 1966 series to score his first Test century in England – a remarkable statistic for such a brilliant batsman.

I did manage to get my century, but only just. I'd hit Lock for a boundary to pass three figures and, next ball, hit a straight drive off the middle of the bat low and like a cannon on the on side. You can imagine my surprise when I saw Lockie dive low on his follow-through to pick up the catch inches from the ground. It was a great catch by a great fielder but ever since, I've pulled Joe Solomon's leg about letting him take it. Joe was the non-striker and, if he had stood his ground, Lockie would never have had the room to make the catch. There's a photo of the dismissal which shows Joe jumping out of the way to allow Lockie room to get down. Ah, well . . .

Thankfully, there were no after-effects from the finger, the doctor had done a good job, and I picked up another half-century in the second innings by which time the West Indies were well on the way to victory. We were all out some time late on the fourth afternoon and it was going through my mind on the field that I would like to use the new ball. For one thing, I knew that England's opener Mickey Stewart was a little suspect against inswerve, my natural ball; for another, we needed to get in as much cricket as possible that afternoon and I would get through the overs more quickly than Wes Hall or Charlie Griffith, our new-ball pair.

But how do you split up one of the most feared fast bowling combinations the game has known? Almost apologetically, I put it to Frank. To my astonishment he said: 'You know, that was just what I was thinking,' and not only did I get the new ball but I bowled the very first over. It took some courage on Frank's part to make that decision since it could have gone all wrong, but he put his faith in me and, luckily, I didn't let him down. The fourth ball left my hand perfectly, the inswinger I was looking for was precisely pitched and Mickey Stewart was bowled all over the place, a vital breakthrough.

We went on to win that match and the series and I felt pretty pleased with life at the end of it. I'd hate to think what would have happened had Freddie Trueman hit me on that finger first ball and put me out of action entirely.

English writer Ron Roberts: 'West Indies' two most brilliant stroke-makers, Kanhai and Sobers, neither of whom had yet made a Test century in this country, and who seldom prosper in partnership, rescued their team with batting of high quality for the third wicket.

'. . . The character of the play after lunch, however, took on a different tone as first Kanhai, then Sobers, whose septic finger gave seemingly little discomfort, established themselves with strokes of vivid design and exciting execution. Kanhai is often an impetuous little man but he has the flair for the big occasion and his judgment this day, when he had given vent to this initial nervous impulse, was well-nigh faultless.

'Sobers also played himself in with studied care and impeccable taste. Then, when Titmus came on, he opened up with a withering broadside of perfectly timed sweeps.

'. . . Lock struck by having Sobers caught and bowled, low and

England v West Indies, Leeds, 1963 (4th Test)

West Indies

C. C. Hunte	c Parks b Trueman	22	b Trueman	4
E. D. A. St J. McMorris	c Barrington b Shackleton	11	lbw b Trueman	1
R. B. Kanhai	b Lock	92	lbw b Shackleton	44
B. F. Butcher	c Parks b Dexter	23	c Dexter b Shackleton	78
G. St A. Sobers	c and b Lock	102	c Sharpe b Titmus	52
J. S. Solomon	c Stewart b Trueman	62	c Titmus b Shackleton	16
D. L. Murray†	lbw b Titmus	34	c Lock b Titmus (8)	2
F. M. M. Worrell*	c Close b Lock	25	c Parks b Titmus (7)	0
W. W. Hall	c Shackleton b Trueman	15	c Trueman b Titmus	7
C. C. Griffith	c Stewart b Trueman	1	not out	12
L. R. Gibbs	not out	0	c Sharpe b Lock	6
Extras	(B 4, LB 5, W 1)	10	(LB 7)	7
Total		**397**		**229**

England

M. J. Stewart	c Gibbs b Griffith	2	b Sobers	0
J. B. Bolus	c Hunte b Hall	14	c Gibbs b Sobers	43
E. R. Dexter*	b Griffith	8	lbw b Griffith	10
K. F. Barrington	c Worrell b Gibbs	25	lbw b Sobers	32
D. B. Close	b Griffith	0	c Solomon b Griffith	56
P. J. Sharpe	c Kanhai b Griffith	0	c Kanhai b Gibbs	13
J. M. Parks†	c Gibbs b Griffith	22	lbw b Gibbs	57
F. J. Titmus	lbw b Gibbs	33	st Murray b Gibbs	5
F. S. Trueman	c Hall b Gibbs	4	c Griffith b Gibbs	5
G. A. R. Lock	b Griffith	53	c Murray b Griffith	1
D. Shackleton	not out	1	not out	1
Extras	(B 4, LB 6, NB 2)	12	(B 3, LB 5)	8
Total		**174**		**231**

England	O	M	R	W		O	M	R	W
Trueman	46	10	117	4		13	1	46	2
Shackleton	42	10	88	1		26	2	63	3
Dexter	23	4	68	1		2	0	15	0
Titmus	25	5	60	1		19	2	44	4
Lock	28.4	9	54	3		7.1	0	54	1

West Indies	O	M	R	W		O	M	R	W
Hall	13	2	61	1		5	1	12	0
Griffith	21	5	36	6		18	5	45	3
Gibbs	14	2	50	3		37.4	12	76	4
Sobers	6	1	15	0		32	5	90	3

wide and hard to his left, a catch of wonderment even by Lock's standards. Sobers, who had just completed a four-hour century (no English batsman has yet done this in the series) could not believe the evidence of his own eyes and stood there dazed before he accepted he was out.'

(Reproduced from *Playfair Cricket Monthly*, September 1963.)

13 Captain and Controversy

West Indies v Australia, Kingston, 1965

It seems I keep coming back to Sabina Park, the Test ground in Kingston, Jamaica, but it was there that so many of the best of my days occurred. It was the scene of my debut Test century, that record 365 not out against Pakistan, and, in all, I made a lot of runs and took quite a few wickets as well there. It was also at Sabina Park that I captained the West Indies for the first time in a Test match.

To be honest, I had never given much serious thought to becoming West Indies captain. Before Frank Worrell finally was appointed for the 1960–61 series in Australia, the captaincy had gone to amateurs from the upper class – and I was neither amateur nor upper-class! Surely, it was beyond me.

However, things were changing in the West Indies, politically and socially, and Frank had a tremendous impact with the success he made of the captaincy, the first black West Indian in that position. He took over from Gerry Alexander and, in Australia, Gerry served as his deputy. When Gerry retired after that Australian tour, Conrad Hunte was appointed vice-captain.

Although Frank consulted with me on cricket matters several times, especially during the 1963 tour of England, it didn't occur to me that the West Indies Board would look beyond Conrad when Frank retired. After all, he was vice-captain. He was also very heavily involved with Moral Re-Armament, known as MRA, the Christian organization, and this led some people to believe that he was not as fully

79

committed to his cricket as he might have been. When he had gone through a bad patch with the bat, one reporter wrote that MRA stood not only for Moral Re-Armament but, in Conrad's case, 'More Runs Available'.

Frank called it a day after the 1963 tour of England but, since the West Indies didn't have their next series scheduled until 1965, at home against Australia, there was no rush over the appointment of his successor. Naturally, there was a lot of speculation in the press and, more and more, I found that I was emerging as favourite. Eventually, a letter arrived at Norton, where I was playing in the North Staffordshire League early in the 1964 season, offering me the captaincy. It took me a little time before I could write to them and accept the invitation. I don't know why I thought it over so long. Perhaps I was in a state of shock over the prospect of yours truly, always one of the rank and file, suddenly rising to be the commander of the troops.

I had never captained any team in my life but I reckoned that I must have picked up something playing as much as I had over the years.

At the end of that season, Frank – *Sir* Frank since the Queen had knighted him in her New Year's Honours list of 1964 – assembled a team of West Indians from the leagues and county scene to play a series of matches against an England side. In the last match at Lord's he came across and said in that casual way of his, 'Well, you'll be skipper of the West Indies from now on, so how about starting here.' It was the first time in my life I had led a team on the field and, as fate would have it, rain restricted play to one of the three days.

The real thing would come some months later in the cricketing cauldron that is Sabina Park against the tough Australians. It would be, everyone in the West Indies kept saying, for the 'championship of the world'. Under Frank we had beaten India 5–0 and England 3–1 in our previous two series and victory over Australia would make us champions.

My last Test – at Lord's, 1973 – fighting England and an injured knee

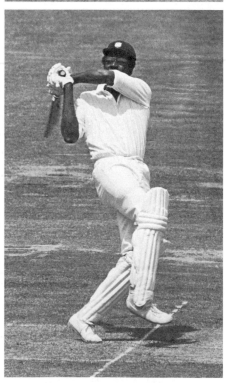

This time, bowling for my English county, Nottinghamshire

FACING PAGE

Four West Indies captains – Sir Frank Worrell (*top left*), Rohan Kanhai (*top right*),
myself (*bottom left*) and Clive Lloyd

Enjoying Malcolm Nash's bowling in the match against Glamorgan at Swansea in 1968, and the six sixes in an over

Left: Charlie Griffiths and Wes Hall – it was a pleasure to have them on one's side

Dennis Lillee and Jeff Thomson (*below*), with Lillee in action (*right*), answered the West Indies pace attack with some fire of their own

Left: Jim Laker, together with Tony Lock, must certainly figure in my list of memorable opponents

Sharing memories with Ray Lindwall (centre) and Neil Harvey

New Zealand and Pakistan, whom we hadn't played for some time, somehow didn't seem to come into the reckoning! I was under no illusions about how tough it would be but I did have an advantage or two. For one thing, Frank Worrell remained on as manager of the team so that I always had his knowledge and advice to fall back on. He had been a great influence on all of us during his tenure and, even though he consciously tried to remain in the background in his new position, his presence was a comfort. For another, I was handed a strong, well-knit team including the greats of the day – Hunte, Nurse, Kanhai, Butcher, Solomon, Hendriks, Hall, Griffith and Gibbs. To top it off, the first Test was at Sabina, a ground where I felt I could do anything.

I knew a lot of attention would be on me to see how I would handle the new job. The papers were full of speculation on how the captaincy would affect my performances, how the players would accept me, what Frank's role would be and so on. The Australians were a powerful team who, under the captaincy of Bobby Simpson, had just beaten England in England the previous summer and had never lost a series against us.

After the first day's play, we were struggling: all out 239, Australia 30-odd without loss and Simpson and Lawry in. However, I knew they would have difficulty coping with Hall and Griffith on a typically hard, fast Sabina pitch. As always, it was prepared so that it had such a shine on it, you could see your reflection. 'Hey, I think I'll shave out here tomorrow morning,' Neil Hawke cracked when he saw it. It really was an extraordinary sight – and one to make any fast bowler's eyes light up.

It was the type of pitch on which I might have sent in the opposition later in my career, but this was my first Test and I didn't think I should be that dramatic. Still, it kept its pace all the way through, Hall and Griffith bowled fast and magnificently and we went on to win the match by 179 runs.

Personally, I didn't achieve much. My movements were restricted by a strained thigh muscle and I found I couldn't run freely or stretch forward comfortably while batting. But Sabina Park couldn't let me leave without some personal landmark to remember the match by – quite apart from the memorable one of victory in my first Test as captain – for when I had Peter Philpott caught at leg-slip by Rohan Kanhai, it was my 100th Test wicket.

Unfortunately, that Test and the whole series was overshadowed by a controversy over Charlie Griffith's action. Richie Benaud, armed with what seemed like hundreds of photographs, caused quite a sensation on the third day of the match by writing in his newspaper reports that Griff's action was illegal – that he was a chucker. There had been talk of Griff throwing since he had once been no-balled by Barbadian umpire Cortez Jordan in a match against India in 1962. It had been repeated in England on our tour in 1963 and now Richie, a former Australian Test captain, stirred up the pot to boiling point again.

I was never one to get into controversies and, as captain, I told Charlie to disregard all the talk and just bowl. He had not been called in England and they were the best umpires in the world. He had, in fact, only been called once in his life. In short, I said, leave it to the umpires. I know that was easier said than done and chucking controversies have always led to a lot of bitterness. That one certainly spoiled that series, to the extent that the Australians were obsessed with it and the spirit of the great 1960–61 tour was missing.

Not that this mattered to the cricket fans of the West Indies. We followed that first Test victory with another in the third and clinched our first-ever series against Australia by comfortably drawing the fourth Test at Kensington Oval in Barbados. 'World champions,' they proclaimed, and it was a distinctly happy feeling in my very first time out as captain – even if we did lose the final Test by ten wickets. It was probably just the morning after the night before – figuratively speaking, of course!

West Indies v Australia, Kingston, 1964–65 (1st Test)

West Indies

Batsman	1st innings		2nd innings	
C. C. Hunte	c Grout b Philpott	41	c Simpson b Mayne	81
S. M. Nurse	c Grout b Hawke	15	run out	17
R. B. Kanhai	c Philpott b McKenzie	17	c and b Philpott	16
B. F. Butcher	b Mayne	39	c Booth b Philpott	71
G. St A. Sobers*	lbw b Simpson	30	c Simpson b Philpott (6)	27
J. S. Solomon	c Grout b Mayne	0	c Grout b Mayne (7)	76
J. L. Hendriks†	b Philpott	11	b O'Neill (8)	30
A. W. White	not out	57	st Grout b Philpott (9)	3
W. W. Hall	b Hawke	9	b Mayne (10)	16
C. C. Griffith	b Mayne	6	not out (11)	1
L. R. Gibbs	b Mayne	6	b Mayne (5)	5
Extras	(B 4, LB 3, W 1)	8	(B 20, LB 7, W 1, NB 2)	30
Total		**239**		**373**

Australia

Batsman	1st innings		2nd innings	
W. M. Lawry	lbw b Hall	19	b Griffith	17
R. B. Simpson*	c Kanhai b Hall	11	c Hendriks b Hall	16
R. M. Cowper	c Nurse b Hall	26	lbw b Hall (4)	2
N. C. O'Neill	c Butcher b White	40	c Nurse b Gibbs (5)	22
B. C. Booth	b Griffith	2	b Griffith (6)	56
G. Thomas	b Griffith	23	b Hall (7)	15
P. I. Philpott	c White b Hall	22	c Kanhai b Sobers (8)	9
N. J. N. Hawke	not out	45	b Solomon (3)	33
A. T. W. Grout†	c Nurse b Hall	5	lbw b Hall	2
G. D. McKenzie	b White	0	c Hill b White	20
L. C. Mayne	b Sobers	9	not out	11
Extras	(B 2, LB 8, NB 5)	15	(NB 13)	13
Total		**217**		**216**

Australia	O	M	R	W	O	M	R	W
McKenzie	20	2	70	1	33	7	56	0
Hawke	14	4	47	2	18	5	25	0
Mayne	17.2	2	43	4	23.4	5	56	4
Philpott	14	2	56	2	47	10	109	4
Simpson	4	2	15	1	15	2	36	0
Cowper					9	1	27	0
O'Neill					7	0	34	1

West Indies	O	M	R	W	O	M	R	W
Hall	24	0	60	5	19	5	45	4
Griffith	20	2	59	2	14	3	36	2
Sobers	20.4	7	30	1	17	2	64	1
Gibbs	16	8	19	0	9	1	21	1
White	15	4	34	2	14.5	8	14	1
Solomon					5	0	23	1

Rohan Kanhai: 'We did it, I'm convinced, because of the remarkable maturing of Gary Sobers. Some people, obviously not in the know, were sceptical that we would fall apart at the seams without Frank Worrell's leadership on the field. Well, it didn't work out that way and Frank knew it wouldn't.

'He'd been around too long for his influence and know-how not to rub off on every member of the side. Gary was the obvious one to carry on in the Worrell vein . . . he's shrewd, popular, a deep thinker and a good leader. With Frank appointed team manager (a thing never before done for a home series) the leadership was strengthened, not weakened.

'To me Gary is the world's top all-rounder, but the extra responsibility the skipper's job brought made him an even greater cricketer. Before he would go out to make a hundred flashy runs. Now he dropped himself down the order and went out with the idea of grafting for runs if necessary. His mental approach to the game had completely changed.'

(Reproduced from *Blasting For Runs*, 1966.)

14 That Old Black Magic

Barbados v Guyana, Bridgetown, 1966

It may sound unbelievable but I probably played more matches for Nottinghamshire in a single season in the 1970s than I did in my whole career for my native Barbados. One of these days I'll have a statistician check for me exactly how many matches I did play for Barbados but I'm sure they weren't many more than thirty.

It wasn't that I didn't care to play more. I was as keen to do well for Barbados as I was in a Test match but I was a professional cricketer, the game was my life and I often found that Barbados' matches clashed with my seasons for South Australia or else coincided with West Indies tours overseas. In addition, in my early days, there was no regular inter-territorial tournament, as there has been since 1966 with the Shell Shield. In fact, some years Barbados wouldn't have a match at all.

I never could understand what the problem was in organizing a West Indian tournament, since it seemed to be so essential to the development of our cricket. Fortunately, the West Indies Board began to see it that way too in the 1960s and several tournaments were arranged. Then Shell came along to sponsor the Shield, which has been an annual event since 1966, bringing together all the cricket-playing territories.

That inaugural season I happened to be there and I led the Barbados team to the championship both in 1966 and again in 1967. Our cricket has always been strong; the people take a real pride in the quality of their cricketers and it would

85

be hard to match the eleven we put in the field in that first season of the Shield.

The West Indies team went to England right afterwards and no fewer than nine Barbadians were included in the seventeen, eight from the Shield team. The odd man out was Wes Hall, who couldn't play because he was recovering from injury. The other eight who were in our championship team were myself, Conrad Hunte, Seymour Nurse, Peter Lashley, Rawle Brancker, David Holford, wicket-keeper David Allan and Charlie Griffith. Our opening batsman Robin Bynoe had a wonderful season and must have been very close to selection, going to India later in the year. Fast bowler Richard Edward missed out because of injury but went to Australia and New Zealand with the West Indies a few years later and even the youngest member, off-spinner Tony Howard, later played Test cricket for the West Indies.

In my experience, not many teams could compare with Barbados' strength that season. Perhaps the great New South Wales sides of the 1960s, with a similar number of Test players, would have been as strong. What matches they would have been!

It was no wonder that Barbados won two of the four games that season by an innings and a third by seven wickets. And it wasn't that the opposition was light. Let us take the match against Guyana as an example, because that captures the quality of West Indian domestic cricket at the time – and also the fierce rivalry that it engendered. We might have had a powerful all-round team but you couldn't exactly describe the Guyanese as a pushover. From No. 3 to No. 6 they batted, in order, Rohan Kanhai, Basil Butcher, Joe Solomon and a gangling, young left-hander in glasses by the name of Clive Lloyd. If you look in *Wisden*, you'll see all four figure prominently among West Indian Test batting records.

If they had no fast bowler of note, their captain that season, Lance Gibbs, was an off-spinner without peer in my experience and he was complemented by a very good left-arm orthodox spinner, Edwin Mohammed, who although he never actually played for the West Indies was certainly of Test standard. With two such teams lined up against each other, a stirring battle was guaranteed. But there was a little more to it than just the array of talent on display. Barbados and Guyana had been the top teams in the West Indies throughout the 1960s and Barbados had usually come out second best. Barbadians were still smarting from the humiliation of 1963, when the Guyanese came to Kensington Oval and Gibbs, with ten wickets in the match, and Mohammed routed us in the second innings for 98 to win by 34 runs.

Barbados' batting in that match was pretty formidable on paper, led by the great Everton Weekes and including other Test players in Cammie Smith, Nurse and Lashley. Yet they were actually 68 for nine before the last pair saved some face. Luckily, I was in Australia playing Shield cricket at the time but I heard later that every batsman came back into the dressing-room with some excuse for failure that day. Someone heard a no-ball called, someone else was distracted by a butterfly on the pitch, yet another got something in his eye. It is a match which has become part of West Indian cricket legend.

Guyana had come back to Barbados the following season and Gibbs and Mohammed again caused problems but we had managed to hold on for a draw. To Barbadians, this spin combination loomed large like a pair of cricketing witch doctors. So the stage was set for the 1966 clash, again at Kensington, and the Guyanese came prepared to dish out the same old black magic. In addition to Gibbs and Mohammed, they brought along another left-arm spinner, Rex Collymore, a tall lad who used his height well and who got into the West Indies team to India later that year.

I may have been in Australia when all the earlier humiliation was suffered but I wasn't left in any doubt what this match meant to Barbadians. I was back home and as captain too and I was told – by Board members, by selectors, by players, by nutsellers, by groundsmen – that we just couldn't let it happen again. With that combination, you would have expected Barbados to have beaten most teams but there was a feeling of pessimism around. It's amazing what defeat can do to destroy confidence.

Guyana – known then as British Guiana since it had not yet become a nation in its own right – batted first and Charlie Griffith started off like a hurricane. Charlie was an extremely dangerous bowler when he put his mind to it for he had real speed, a wicked bouncer and the complementary ball, the yorker, down into the boots. He was a big man who did not smile much and presented a daunting figure to opposing batsmen – who would have known what St George felt like facing the dragon.

In no time, Griff got rid of Steve Camacho, then a young opener who later played for the West Indies and who has since become secretary to the West Indies Board, and then turned his attention on Vincent Mayers, a little opener, no more than 5 feet 2 inches tall. I had the feeling that the fury was meant more for Kanhai than little Mayersie for Charlie still remembered a century by Rohan when they last met in Barbados two years earlier. I wasn't there to see it but I've heard enough of it to know it was a typically brilliant Kanhai performance. They say he just kept hooking and driving Griffith and Wes Hall all over the ground: no mean feat.

Rohan, of course, could handle himself but it was a little different with his diminutive partner. How he got out of the way of a few of Charlie's firebolts I'll never know and I'm sure he was glad when he was out. They say he packed his bags right after that match and emigrated to the US!

Kanhai and Butcher put on over 100 but the total was only 227. As long as we could get over this inferiority complex about Gibbs and Mohammed it was nothing to worry about – not with our batting. When I went in, early on the second day, Seymour Nurse had just been dismissed and we were 90-odd for three. Lance was on and he knew, and I knew, that this would be the crucial part of the match. Would he and Mohammed dominate us again – or could we break free?

I was determined that, whatever else, I wouldn't be pinned

down. Lance was an attacking bowler, probing, spinning, varying, and my policy was to meet attack with attack. I was on about 30 when the policy should have finished me off. Moving out to drive, I was beaten in the air and was so sure I'd be stumped that I didn't even bother to try to get back in. The pavilion was at the bowler's end and I was walking towards it when I realized the wicket-keeper hadn't gathered the ball.

So I simply turned around and put my bat back behind the crease while he fumbled around searching in vain for the lost cherry. By this time, the smoke was coming out of Lance's ears. He was one of the most competitive cricketers I've ever known. He played it hard and expected everyone else to play it hard too. He just couldn't stand sloppiness on the field and this was an easy chance. What is more, it was a vital one; Lance was the offended bowler and also captain.

A youngster by the name of Jackman was the keeper and this was his first season. I think it was also his last. Lance let him have a few choice words which, freely translated, went something like, 'You know who you've let off. He isn't exactly a rabbit. You know we're going to pay for your incompetence.' In the vernacular it sounded a lot worse and poor Jackman went to pieces.

Unfortunately for him, Guyana did pay. Conditions were good and I put my head down, making up my mind to win this particular battle. I had century-partnerships with Lashley and Brancker, two other left-handers – which was significant because I don't believe Lance particularly cared for bowling to left-handers. By the time Lance had Brancker, a good, steady all-round cricketer, the total was over 400.

In the end, I made a double-hundred, 204, and Barbados totalled 559 for nine declared. Rawle's was Lance's only wicket, Edwin Mohammed didn't get a wicket at all and Barbados finally laid to rest the Guyana bogey. We went on to win the match by an innings but two incidents stick in my mind about the Guyana second innings. The first was Basil Butcher's dismissal. He came in with Charlie Griffith bowling at great pace, having got rid of both Camacho and poor Vincent Mayers with fearsome bouncers. Butcher was struck on the pad first ball and, without waiting for the umpire's decision, walked off. It's the only time I've seen a batsman walk on an lbw decision. Butch, an outstanding Test batsman, had scored 99 in the first innings but this time he didn't show much interest in sticking around with Griffith in that mood!

The second feature was a magnificent century by Clive Lloyd. He was then not yet twenty and the Guyana manager, Berkeley Gaskin, had arrived singing his praises. I got him in the first innings leg before and, afterwards, pulled Berkeley's leg about it – but he had the last laugh. Clive, as ungainly as he looked with his spectacles and stoop-shouldered walk, hit the ball hard and often, and reeled off a tremendous century. It wasn't hard then to see why Berkeley had spoken so highly of him nor to realize that he would go far in West Indies cricket. In addition, he gave a wonderful exhibition of fielding in the covers.

These days the territories in the West Indies can't often field full strength teams in the Shield because there are more opportunities for playing professionally in Australia and, more recently, South Africa, during the Caribbean season. In addition, their cricketers play so much now that many of them are keen to rest in the Shield. Even so, the rivalry remains intense and I'm sure that, whoever is playing, they are every bit as committed to knocking the neighbouring team off as we were to beating the Guyanese in that first Shield season in 1966.

Barbadian writer Clyde Walcott: 'The full power of the heavy Barbados batting machinery was demonstrated as British Guiana's bowlers worked all day for only two successes.

'Appropriately enough, the man at the helm of operations was skipper Garfield Sobers who, with an undefeated double century, steered his team's batting with purpose and application which more than compensated for his loss of the toss.

Barbados v Guyana, Bridgetown, 1966

Guyana

S. Camacho	c Holford b Griffith	5	c Lashley b Griffith	13
V. Mayers	c Bynoe b Griffith	2	c Hunte b Griffith	8
R. B. Kanhai	c Allan b Sobers	69	b Howard	43
B. F. Butcher	c Nurse b Sobers	99	lbw b Griffith	0
J. S. Solomon	c Allan b Griffith	28	c Allan b Edwards	70
C. Lloyd	lbw b Sobers	0	b Howard	107
R. Ramnarace	lbw b Holford	0	run out	6
C. Collymore	b Sobers	5	lbw b Holford	20
S. Jackman†	c Bynoe b Sobers	5	b Holford	10
E. Mohammed	not out	5	b Griffith	9
L. R. Gibbs*	lbw b Sobers	3	not out	8
Extras	(W 2, NB 4)	6	(B 9, LB 10, W 1, NB 3)	23
Total		**227**		**317**

Barbados

C. C. Hunte	c Butcher b Solomon	9
M. R. Bynoe	c Collymore b Solomon	8
S. M. Nurse	st Jackman b Collymore	52
P. Lashley	b Collymore	54
G. St A. Sobers*	c Jackman b Solomon	204
R. Brancker	b Gibbs	132
D. Holford	c Collymore b Solomon	11
D. W. Allan†	run out	1
C. C. Griffith	lbw b Ramnarace	38
A. Howard	not out	9
R. Edwards	not out	6
Extras	(B 7, LB 27, W 1)	35
Total	(9 wickets declared)	**559**

Barbados	O	M	R	W		O	M	R	W
Griffith	11	3	28	3		15.5	2	49	4
Edwards	7	2	26	0		16	2	43	1
Sobers	21.3	6	56	6		18	4	82	0
Holford	19	2	49	1		26	7	53	2
Howard	3	0	22	0		22	7	56	2
Brancker	10	2	40	0					
Nurse						3	0	11	0
Lashley						1	1	0	0

Guyana	O	M	R	W
Ramnarace	31	7	112	1
Solomon	13	1	46	4
Gibbs	62	16	111	1
Mohammed	31	6	97	0
Collymore	51	11	154	2
Lloyd	1	0	4	0

Gary Sobers' Most Memorable Matches

'With Dame Fortune favouring him, Sobers, hitting with great power, was associated with two very fruitful partnerships with Peter Lashley and Rawle Brancker which were of vital importance to his team.

'The day started on a bright note for British Guiana when Seymour Nurse whose stroking of the ball on Friday evening appeared menacing indeed, was brilliantly stumped by wicket-keeper Sydney Jackman off the first delivery from tall left-hander Rex Collymore with only two added to the overnight total of 94.

'But this show of brilliance didn't serve Jackman any length of time and, in less than an hour, he must have been the most dejected man in the middle, having missed a stumping chance Sobers offered at 21 off Lance Gibbs and a catching chance which the batsman offered 20 runs later.'

(Reproduced from the *Sunday Advocate*, Barbados, 20 February 1966.)

15 At Home on a True Brown Top

West Indies v England, Lord's, 1966

When I'm old and grey – or should it be older and greyer? – and I'm sitting in my rocking chair recalling happy days on the cricket field, the summer of 1966 will figure prominently in my thoughts.

The West Indies toured England in that year; it was the first time I was captain on an overseas tour and it turned out to be a dream season for the team and for me personally. It seemed as if I could do nothing wrong, almost as if someone up there were making sure I was looked after.

I called the toss correctly in all five Tests (it was 'heads' every time by the way), I had over 700 runs in the series, took 20 wickets and held a few catches as well. What was even more important, we won the series 3–1 and only a defeat in the last Test at the Oval by an innings spoiled things a little.

It was also the summer of the innings which for several reasons has given me the greatest satisfaction of all in my Test career: 163 not out at Lord's in the second Test. We had won the first Test up at Old Trafford by an innings in three days, a repeat of our victory there in the 1963 Test. Again we batted first, Conrad Hunte and myself made centuries and then Lance Gibbs, with five wickets in each innings, bowled them out.

We'd had the better conditions because the pitch did favour spin more and more and there was no question that we had a superb team, probably the best-balanced West Indies team in my experience. Yet England panicked after that defeat,

changed captains, replacing Mike Smith with Colin Cowdrey, and brought in a few new faces for the Lord's Test. I thought at the time that it was rough on Mike Smith who had just had a good tour in Australia and who was hardly to blame for the collapse of their batting. But he had failed with the bat and out he went.

When we were 95 for five just before lunch on the Monday, the fourth day of the match, England's selection seemed fully justified. The state of play then was that we had been bowled out for 269, to which England had replied with 355, a somewhat elderly gentleman by the name of Tom Graveney marking his return to Test cricket with 96. How England could have left out this most elegant of batsmen for so long when he would have been at the height of his career, I'll never be able to understand.

That put them ahead by 86 which meant that when David Holford came in to join me at the fall of the fifth wicket in our second innings we were only nine ahead, with just our keeper, David Allan, Wes Hall, Charlie Griffith and Lance Gibbs to follow. We were in a spot of bother, I suppose you might say.

The route from the ground to the dressing rooms at Lord's carries you through the famous Long Room past the bar and up a flight of stairs, which means past hundreds of MCC members. When I came back in at lunch that day, the faces were beaming in expectation of certain victory. The colours on the MCC ties seemed to be positively shining!

As far as I was concerned, the match was far from over but there again, as I think you may have gathered, I'm the eternal optimist. Yet I knew David could bat. He is my first cousin, the bright one in the family with a university degree and with a calm head on his shoulders. He'd played pretty well on the tour and we'd put on over 100 in the Old Trafford Test.

All well and good but the situation was somewhat different now. Here was a young player, in only his second Test, Lord's at that, with the West Indies in trouble and England's bowlers with their tails in the air. He would be the centre of attention early on, not me, for I had to decide the best way to bring him on and Colin had to decide what tactics he would use now.

I'd been criticized, before and since, for batting too low in the order, at No. 6, but there is no occasion I can recall when I've run out of partners – and several when my presence with the lower order has made the difference, as it did now. I've always felt that it is wrong to try to shield your partner, no matter where he's batting in the order, for it gives him a sense of inferiority, and insecurity. Certainly David was capable of handling himself.

Colin's policy, fortunately, suited me perfectly. He opted to crowd me at first but, after I had deliberately counter-attacked, he pushed the field back and offered me the single to get at David. I said 'thank you very much', took the runs that were there and let David take his share of the responsibility. I'm sure this helped to bring out the best in him, while I was happy that I could settle in without much pressure.

There was one piece of advice I gave to David early in the partnership. 'Look at this pitch,' I told him. 'It's just like a Kensington pitch, isn't it? Do you really feel there's anybody who can get you out if you put your head down on this?' In fact, it was very similar in appearance to the pitches we get at home at Kensington Oval in Barbados, a true brown top, and it played beautifully all the way through. So did David and he went from strength to strength – and I like to feel that the reference to Barbados made him relax more and feel at home.

We batted right through until close of play that day and then into the final day and when David had made a really wonderful century, we were in a position which allowed me to declare. The equation then was 284 runs to win for them, four hours to win for us. If they could get them, good luck to them, but my concern was for us to bowl them out.

When we had got rid of Boycott, Barrington, Cowdrey and

Parks for 60-odd it looked very much as if we would. In the end, we couldn't get past the weighty figure of Colin Milburn (who hit the ball as only he could in getting a memorable century) and the experienced Graveney and we had to settle for a draw.

Why do I rate this the best innings I've played in Tests? Primarily because of the state of the game, knowing that if I had got out at any time it would probably have opened the way to an England victory. Simultaneously, I had to think of my attitude to an inexperienced partner at the other end, trying to give him confidence. Then there was the tactical battle with Cowdrey. He crowded me at first, to which my response was an immediate and deliberate counter-attack. Perhaps he was a little timid, for after a few strokes he pushed his men back and eased the pressure. The first round had been won and, in the end, nearly the bout. Yes, the summer of 1966 – and especially the Lord's Test – is a memory I'll always cherish.

English writer Brian Scovell: 'Sobers, naturally, took on the role of senior partner but Holford was so determined, so correct, that there was really no need to shield him. Cowdrey crowded Holford with fielders whereas he put his men out to Sobers.

'In the next morning's newspapers this tactic came under devastating fire, particularly from Keith Miller in the *Daily Express*. Cowdrey's idea was to get Sobers away from the bowling to get at Holford. All he succeeded in doing was to give Sobers a lot of easy runs he would have had to work hard for and save him the anxiety of having to cope with an attacking field.

'Cowdrey worked on the principle that Sobers in this grim mood was unshiftable so let's get the break against the inexperienced (this was only his second Test after only six first-class games of cricket in the West Indies) 27-year-old Holford. As it turned out, Sobers was unshiftable but no one knows what would have happened had he had more pressure put on him.'

(Reproduced from *Everything That's Cricket*.)

England v West Indies, Lord's, 1966 (2nd Test)

West Indies

C. C. Hunte	c Parks b Higgs	18	c Milburn b Knight	13 '
M. C. Carew	c Parks b Higgs	2	c Knight b Higgs	0
R. B. Kanhai	c Titmus b Higgs	25	c Parks b Knight	40
B. F. Butcher	c Milburn b Knight	49	lbw b Higgs	3
S. M. Nurse	b D'Oliveira	64	c Parks b D'Oliveira	35
G. St A. Sobers*	lbw b Knight	46	not out	163
D. A. J. Holford	b Jones	26	not out	105
D. W. Allan†	c Titmus b Higgs	13		
C. C. Griffith	lbw b Higgs	5		
W. W. Hall	not out	8		
L. R. Gibbs	c Parks b Higgs	4		
Extras	(B 2, LB 7)	9	(LB 8, NB 2)	10
Total		**269**	(5 wickets declared)	**369**

England

G. Boycott	c Griffith b Gibbs	60	c Allan b Griffith	25
C. Milburn	lbw b Hall	6	not out	126
T. W. Graveney	c Allan b Hall	96	not out (6)	30
K. F. Barrington	b Sobers	19	b Griffith (3)	5
M. C. Cowdrey*	c Gibbs b Hall	9	c Allan b Hall (4)	5
J. M. Parks†	lbw b Carew	91	b Hall (5)	0
B. L. D'Oliveira	run out	27		
B. R. Knight	b Griffith	6		
F. J. Titmus	c Allan b Hall	6		
K. Higgs	c Holford b Gibbs	13		
I. J. Jones	not out	0		
Extras	(B 7, LB 10, NB 5)	22	(B4 LB 2)	6
Total		**355**	(4 wickets)	**197**

England	O	M	R	W	O	M	R	W
Jones	21	3	64	1	25	2	95	0
Higgs	33	9	91	6	34	5	82	2
Knight	21	0	63	2	30	3	106	2
Titmus	5	0	18	0	19	3	30	0
D'Oliveira	14	5	24	1	25	7	46	1
West Indies								
Sobers	39	12	89	1	8	4	8	0
Hall	36	2	106	4	14	1	65	2
Griffith	28	4	79	1	11	2	43	2
Gibbs	37.3	18	48	2	13	4	40	0
Carew	3	0	11	1				
Holford					9	1	35	0

16 The Six Sixes
Nottinghamshire v Glamorgan, Swansea, 1968

The year 1968 was an historic one for English cricket. It was the year they decided to allow the counties to register one overseas player immediately and without any residential qualification as had previously been the case. There had been a strong move for some time to bring in the best international players and the impact was immediate and beneficial and, I personally believe, has been so ever since, even though some questions are being raised in England about the number of those now playing.

I had been approached some years before about whether I would accept a county contract but I wasn't willing to sit out the residential qualification period and miss Test cricket. The same was true of a number of others but, once the gates were opened, several of us joined the county scene. Rohan Kanhai went to Warwickshire, Asif Iqbal to Kent, Majid Khan to Glamorgan, Barry Richards to Hampshire, Farouk Engineer to Lancashire and so on. I went to Nottinghamshire, a surprise to many people since it was a county which had been wallowing near the bottom of the championship for many seasons.

To be frank, it was a question of the highest bidder making a deal with my agent but when I heard that I'd be going to Notts I was particularly pleased. For one thing, I knew the Trent Bridge wicket to be one of the best in England – or anywhere else for that matter. After all, the first time I'd played on it, for the West Indies against Notts on the 1957 tour, I made an unbeaten double-century and I scored another big hundred there on the 1966 tour against Notts. More than that, however, was the challenge of trying to pull the Notts side up the championship table.

England were on a tour of the Caribbean at the time and when it was announced I was going to Notts, Bunty Ames, better half of the MCC Manager Les Ames, asked what I thought I'd be able to do. Confidently, I said I thought I could get them in the top four. 'Want to bet on it?' she asked. It was not the kind of challenge I could let pass and, in the end, the wager was for six bottles of champagne that Notts would finish in the first six. The odds on it happening were pretty long, since they'd finished in the bottom three for the past few seasons.

When we started our last match against Glamorgan at Swansea, my ambitions had been almost realized. We were in the top six, I'd made well over 1000 runs and taken over 80 wickets and the world was a lovely place. But we needed points in that game to round off the season perfectly – and to clinch my six bottles of champagne! It was a vital game for Glamorgan, too, since they were even higher than we were in the table and actually had a chance of taking the championship, a rare event for the Welsh county.

There was a big crowd there on the first day, a Saturday, at the St Helen's ground by the sea, a ground also famous for its rugby, but I don't think the home crowds were in such a joyous mood when Brian Bolus made a brilliant century and we passed 300 before our fifth wicket fell. By this time, I was thinking of a declaration as I came in at No. 7 with just the right position to attack.

I'd made 40 and had decided we would bat just one, possibly two, more overs, before declaring to open up the game. Malcolm Nash was on at the time, a left-armer who had opened the bowling at medium-pace and then changed later to bowl spin at something like Derek Underwood's speed. As far as I was concerned at this stage, it was him or me. I wanted as many runs as I could get in the next few minutes and, since there was a short boundary on the leg side, I fancied my chances.

My intention was to swing so hard at each ball that even a mis-hit off the top edge would have cleared the boundary. As it was the first four hit pretty much the centre of the bat and went in various directions on the leg side for sixes. Momentarily forgetting Welsh loyalty, the crowd was quickly caught up in the excitement and was shouting and cheering every stroke.

The fifth ball was slightly wide of my off stump and I didn't quite get hold of it. It went high down to long-off where the fielder went back, caught it – and then fell backwards over the ropes. For what seemed an eternity, confusion reigned. The umpires, John Langridge and Eddie Phillipson, went down to check where the catcher had landed after falling. For myself, I just didn't know whether the catch was clean or not. The law had changed so many times and there was some experimental rule in operation that particular season so I wasn't certain what was what. I was quite prepared to go – although the spectators didn't seem to agree with me: 'six, six' they were shouting – and, eventually, John Langridge lifted his arms to indicate that he concurred with them and I strolled back into the wicket for the last ball.

The crowd was fully aware of its significance. So was Glamorgan captain Tony Lewis, and he dropped almost all his men out. I tried to read Malcolm Nash's mind and anticipated that he would attempt a change of pace to beat my inevitable big hit. Whatever he bowled, I was going to swing and, somehow, he pitched it just to my liking, around middle and leg. I connected perfectly and the ball just soared off the meat of the bat, seemingly further and further out of the ground.

By chance the television cameras, which were covering the match that day, had decided to continue until the end of our innings and so managed to record a piece of cricket history. That particular over has been shown repeatedly ever since and Wilf Wooler's excited comment about the last stroke –

'It's gone clean into Swansea!' – captures the excitement of the moment.

Wilf, of course, was the former Glamorgan captain, Welsh rugby union international and a great personality in both sports. When we arrived at the ground on the Monday, a small boy came up to him with a ball. 'Could this be the ball that Mr Sobers hit for six Saturday?' he asked. It was, and when Wilf asked him where he had found it, he replied: 'Well, it was still rolling down the road when I picked it up!' It was later specially mounted and sent to the Trent Bridge cricket museum. Whatever happened to the bat I used that day I'm not sure, although I understand that at least ten bats that hit those six sixes have since been raffled.

I've always felt a little sorry for Malcolm Nash in all of this for, let us be honest, six sixes in a single over really is something of a freak. Over the years, he has been a superb bowler for Glamorgan and must have been close to England selection more than once. Malcolm himself, however, has taken the whole thing in the very best of spirits. We were walking across the ground after that day's play for a television interview and I was a little surprised to find Malcolm as cheerful as he was. 'You seem quite perky for a man who's just been hit for a cricket record,' I said. 'And why not?' he replied. 'You're not the only one who goes into the record books, you know. I do too!'

Nor has it daunted Malcolm's spirit in any way, even after Frank Hayes of Lancashire took five sixes and a four off him in one over at the same St Helen's Ground in 1977. It means that he is now in *Wisden* as the bowler who has conceded not only the highest but the second highest number of runs in a single over. Yet he has kept plugging away and still had a few games for Glamorgan up to the 1983 season.

One of them was against the Sri Lanka World Cup team of which I was coach. When the players saw the name M. A. Nash on the scorecard in the Glamorgan XI, they became quite excited. I think a few of them fancied themselves taking a few sixes off him, but they soon changed their minds when he picked off two quick wickets. 'Hey, he can bowl,' they came back to report.

Yes, records can sometimes be misleading. And if you're wondering, I did collect that champagne from Bunty Ames when we played Kent down at Canterbury a few weeks later. Fittingly there were six bottles as Bunty commented, 'one for each of the sixes!'

Wisden Cricketers' Almanack, 1969: 'This was the history-making match in which the incredible Garfield Sobers created a new world record by hitting six 6s in a six-ball over. Somehow one sensed that something extraordinary was going to happen when Sobers sauntered to the wicket. With over 300 runs on the board for the loss of only five wickets, he had the right sort of platform from which to launch a spectacular assault, and the manner in which he immediately settled down to score at a fast rate was ominous.

'Then came the history-making over by the 23-year-old Malcolm Nash. First crouched like a black panther eager to pounce, Sobers with lightning footwork got into position for a vicious straight drive or pull. As Tony Lewis, Glamorgan's captain, said afterwards, "It was not sheer slogging through strength but scientific hitting with every movement working in harmony."

'Twice the ball was slashed out of the ground and when the last six landed in the street outside it was not recovered until the next day. Then it was presented to Sobers and will have a permanent place in the Trent Bridge Cricket Museum.'

Nottinghamshire v Glamorgan, Swansea, 1968

Nottinghamshire

J. B. Bolus	c sub b Nash	140	run out	3
R. A. White	c Wheatley b B. Lewis	73	b Cordle	1
G. Frost	c A. R. Lewis b Nash	50	b Nash	2
M. J. Smedley	c A. R. Lewis b Nash	27	c Majid b Cordle	24
D. L. Murray†	b Nash	0	c Cordle b Shepherd	13
J. M. Parkin	not out	15	not out	9
G. St A. Sobers*	not out	76	b Shepherd	72
S. R. Bielby	(did not bat)		not out	13
Extras	B 4, LB 7, NB 2)	13	(B 1, NB 1)	2
Total	(5 wickets declared)	**394**	(6 wickets declared)	**139**

Glamorgan

A. Jones	c Murray b Taylor	25	c Parkin b Taylor	1
R. Davis	c Taylor b Stead	0	b Stead	18
Majid Jahangir	c Taylor b Halfyard	41	c Bolus b Taylor	4
A. R. Lewis*	c Bielby b Taylor	0	c Bielby b White	52
P. M. Walker	not out	104	c Sobers b White	16
E. Jones†	lbw b Sobers	29	c Stead b Taylor	3
A. E. Cordle	lbw b Halfyard	4	c Smedley b Taylor	4
M. A. Nash	b Sobers	8	b White	5
B. Lewis	run out	38	b Taylor	4
D. J. Shepherd	c Sobers b Halfyard	0	b White	4
O. S. Wheatley	b White	1	not out	0
Extras	(LB 3, W 1)	4	(LB 2)	2
Total		**254**		**113**

Glamorgan	O	M	R	W	O	M	R	W
Wheatley	5	0	22	0				
Nash	21	3	100	4	17	4	53	1
Cordle	3	1	24	0	16	4	41	2
Walker	32	4	109	0				
Shepherd	25	5	82	0	25	10	43	2
Lewis	13	1	44	1				

Nottinghamshire	O	M	R	W	O	M	R	W
Sobers	20	6	63	2				
Stead	9	3	27	1	9	1	26	1
Taylor	9	2	23	2	16	6	47	5
Halfyard	31	8	71	3	7	1	29	0
White	23.2	5	66	1	8	5	9	4

17 A Devil of a Sabina Pitch

West Indies v England, Kingston, 1968

When you've played cricket for as long as I've done and in so many different countries, you get accustomed to all sorts of pitches. That strip of turf, 22 yards long, is the centrepiece of any cricket match and the way it is prepared and, therefore, the way it plays can determine the outcome.

In my time, I've seen green ones and brown ones and even a pink one, as I mentioned in chapter 5 on the 1957 Test at the Oval. I've played on strips as hard as granite and as soft as putty. I've had to struggle on pitches almost as wet and muddy as a rice paddy and others which have been as dry as the Sahara. And I also played on the pitch at Sabina Park in the 1968 Test against England, one of the most extraordinary I've experienced – both pitch and match.

As long as I had known it, Sabina was always a beautiful batting surface, probably the fastest in the West Indies but always true. Fast bowlers and leg-spinners liked to bowl on it for its pace and bounce but, since the ball came onto the bat and did nothing unpredictable, it was good for batting too. It was there that I played my first Test, scored my record 365 not out against Pakistan and first skippered the West Indies. I liked Sabina and I think Sabina – and its crowds – liked me.

When we arrived at Kingston for the second Test of the 1968 series, we had just managed to force a draw in a tight finish in the first Test in Trinidad. It had meant batting through the final session of play with Wes Hall and I'll never know how we managed! We were something like 20 behind, having followed on, when Wes, at No. 10, joined me just before tea on the final day.

For an over, I watched in disbelief as Wes played with a perfect-looking forward defensive stroke at every ball and missed them all by a good six inches. It was time I had a word with him, I thought, so I went down and told him he was playing down the wrong line completely. 'You know, I thought something was wrong!' he replied – and proceeded to defy the bowlers to the very end. After the game, when the press interviewed us, they asked Wes if he had been worried at any time. 'Well, you know, I wasn't so sure if the fellow at the other end would hold out!' Never at a loss for words, Wes.

Back to Sabina. Since I had last played there, the pitch had been re-laid and there were whispers before the start of that 1968 Test that something had gone wrong. The England boys reported that the strip on which they had played their match against Jamaica had behaved strangely. When we inspected it prior to the start of the Test, it didn't resemble any Sabina wicket I had known. Even before a ball was bowled, it had wide cracks which looked very ominous, although the groundsman said we shouldn't worry about how it looked, only how it played.

His confidence seemed justified when England ended the first day 200-odd for two but it was on the second afternoon that the fun began. The heat of the tropical sun had begun to work on the cracks and they were becoming wider and wider. By the time we went in to bat, you could stick your finger into some and, as you would expect, the ball was starting to do all sorts of strange things.

Nothing fascinates cricketers more than the state of the pitch and we all made our inspections before the start of the third day. Tom Graveney summed things up best when he called across to Lance Gibbs: 'Hey, Lance, you had better not walk across it.' Lance, who hardly cast much of a shadow with his tall, slim figure, didn't get it. 'We wouldn't want you falling into one of those cracks; you might go all the way through to Australia,' Tom said.

It was all right for England to joke. They had batted and they had their runs on the board, 376 of them. We were the ones up against it. On the evening before, Steve Camacho had gone to a shooter – what the Trinidadians call, very descriptively, a 'rat' or a 'snake'. Now Rohan Kanhai was hit on the knuckles by one ball and was digging out a 'rat' the next. Poor Seymour Nurse was hammered about his body and Clive Lloyd got a short one right in the chest. You just didn't know what was coming from one ball to the next.

I came in at 80 for four to face John Snow who, along with David Brown and Jeff Jones, was making things really uncomfortable. They were sharp at the best of times and didn't need this sort of artificial help. I took guard, looked around the field and then went back to play the first ball defensively. Before I could get my bat down, it skidded through, hit me on the boot and I was gone first ball, lbw! It's not a pleasant feeling but I didn't have much time to think about it. Before I knew it, we were all out for 143, more than 230 behind. There wasn't much doubt that Colin Cowdrey would enforce the follow-on on this pitch and soon we were batting again.

I don't think I need to repeat to anyone who has been acquainted with my career that I'm an eternal optimist. This cricket is a funny old game and no match is over until the last ball is bowled, as I had come to realize so often with the West Indies. This time, though, I knew that we needed more than just a little luck to wriggle out.

There is no logical explanation for the turn of events after our first-innings collapse. The long and short of it is that we not only wriggled out but came close to winning in 'extra time' on a sixth day which was only tacked on at England's insistence after crowd troubles had caused an hour-and-a-quarter to be lost on the fourth day.

When we followed on, Seymour Nurse asked me if he could open the innings. We had used Deryck Murray in the first innings as Seymour was not an opener and better suited, we felt, down the order. But now he wanted to open. Sometimes players have these hunches and, since I wasn't happy with Deryck, our keeper, risking injury by batting against the new ball on this pitch, I gladly agreed to Seymour's request.

The result was that he went in and produced some of the most brilliant batting you could wish to see. There was no more stylish player than Seymour and, by close of play, he and Camacho had 80-odd on the board without loss with Seymour well over 50. I don't know if the England bowlers tired or if, by some strange quirk, the pitch lost its devil for a time. Whatever it was, Seymour made it look a different game.

When we started the fourth day, our spirits were up and I felt we were still in with a chance. A few deliveries early on were enough to tell us the pitch had its devil back. Perhaps the intervening rest day in warm sunshine opened up the cracks even more; perhaps the bowlers were fresher. Whatever it was, Camacho and Lloyd were soon bowled by real shooters while in contrast, several balls leapt up throat-high off a length. I came in after Lloyd had gone at 174 for four. Now, I've never had a 'pair' in any form of cricket that I can recall but, that day, I was within a couple of inches of getting one – and a King Pair at that, first ball in each innings.

David Brown was bowling and, remembering what had happened in the first innings, I came forward to the first ball, looking for another shooter. This one did the opposite and bounced sharply from off a length. I could only fend it off; it came off the bat handle and lobbed just over Fred Titmus, fielding bat-pad at forward short leg. Well, I said we needed luck and that incident and one soon after, when Basil d'Oliveira put me down at second slip off Brown when I was on 7 convinced me that Lady Luck was on our side this time. The Great Escape was on. Even so, when Basil Butcher was given out, very legitimately, caught down the leg side by Jim Parks the wicket-keeper, we were five down, still in arrears and with only the all-rounders and bowlers to come.

The crowd riot started at Butch's dismissal. It had been a low catch but a clean one although, as far as some spectators were concerned, not clean enough – not with the West Indies in trouble! Bottles rained onto the field as David Holford came in to replace Butch. Colin Cowdrey and myself went across to try to placate the annoyed spectators and I thought things were settling down when the riot police arrived and stirred them back up again by firing tear gas into the trouble spot. They didn't take into account the direction of the wind and the tear gas didn't hit the bottle-throwers at all but wafted back across the field into the other stands and into the pavilion.

There was mass confusion for some time but when we resumed, David Holford and I batted through the rest of that day and into the next. We added over 100 and I also had good support from Deryck Murray and Charlie Griffith as I went on to a century. Yes, we had our luck but the pitch and the situation had fired my concentration and, as so often happens when the chips are down, I found myself concentrating fiercely. I remember taking twelve singles to move from 88 to 100.

On the field, as our total mounted, I could sense the England team's extreme disappointment and frustration at having another match slip out of their grasp. They were also tired and I knew a declaration would be a further blow to their pride. We were nine wickets down in any case and would hardly have added many more but it put the pressure on them when I closed late in the day, leaving England 159 to win with just under an hour-and-a-half to go, plus the 75 minutes they had asked for to be played on the sixth day.

The press called it cheeky but, on that pitch and in those circumstances, I knew England would only fight for survival. I was convinced that the strange happenings of this strange match were not yet over by any means and I decided to take the new ball myself, in preference to Wes Hall. When I bowled Geoff Boycott and had Cowdrey lbw in my first over, England were manning panic stations.

West Indies v England, Kingston, 1967–68 (2nd Test)

England

G. Boycott	b Hall	17	b Sobers	0
J. H. Edrich	c Kanhai b Sobers	96	b Hall	6
M. C. Cowdrey*	c Murray b Gibbs	101	lbw b Sobers	0
K. F. Barrington	c and b Holford	63	lbw b Griffith	13
T. W. Graveney	b Hall	30	c Griffith b Gibbs	21
J. M. Parks†	c Sobers b Holford	3	lbw b Gibbs	3
B. L. D'Oliveira	st Murray b Holford	0	not out	13
F. J. Titmus	lbw b Hall	19	c Camacho b Gibbs	4
D. J. Brown	c Murray b Hall	14	b Sobers	0
J. A. Snow	b Griffith	10		
I. J. Jones	not out	0		
Extras	(B 12, LB 7, NB 4)	23	(B 8)	8
Total		**376**	(8 wickets)	**68**

West Indies

G. S. Camacho	b Snow	5	b D'Oliveira	25
D. L. Murray†	c D'Oliveira b Brown	0	lbw b Brown (8)	14
R. B. Kanhai	c Graveney b Snow	26	c Edrich b Jones	36
S. M. Nurse	b Jones	22	b Snow (2)	73
C. H. Lloyd	not out	34	b Brown	7
G. St A. Sobers*	lbw b Snow	0	not out	113
B. F. Butcher	c Parks b Snow	21	c Parks b D'Oliveira (4)	25
D. A. J. Holford	c Parks b Snow	6	lbw b Titmus (7)	35
C. C. Griffith	c D'Oliveira b Snow	8	lbw b Jones	14
W. W. Hall	b Snow	0	c Parks b Jones	0
L. R. Gibbs	c Parks b Jones	0	not out	1
Extras	(B 12, LB 5, W 1, NB 3)	21	(B 33, LB 10, NB 5)	48
Total		**143**	(9 wickets declared)	**391**

West Indies	O	M	R	W		O	M	R	W
Hall	27	5	63	4		3	2	3	1
Griffith	31.2	7	72	1		5	2	13	1
Sobers	31	11	56	1		16.5	7	33	3
Gibbs	47	18	91	1		14	11	11	3
Holford	33	10	71	3					

England	O	M	R	W		O	M	R	W
Brown	13	1	34	1		33	9	65	2
Snow	21	7	49	7		27	4	91	1
Jones	14.1	4	39	2		30	4	90	3
D'Oliveira						32	12	51	2
Titmus						7	2	32	1
Barrington						6	1	14	0

By the end of the day, John Edrich and Ken Barrington, those two dour fighters, were also back in the hatch and England, 19 for four, were glad of the fading light that ended play early. Still, they had to come back next morning for the 75 minutes which they had claimed at the time of the crowd troubles. How this was haunting them now! In that time, we grabbed four more wickets, poor Jim Parks received one of the nastiest balls of the match from Wes which leapt at him to hit him on the adam's apple and there was a lot of playing and missing, appealing and tension.

Yet we just couldn't complete what would have been one of the most amazing victories in Test cricket. Fortunately, when we played again at Sabina, that 'horror pitch' had been re-laid and, this time, they got it right. And I'm glad to say that Lance Gibbs took Tom Graveney's advice and he never did get too close to any of those cracks.

Former Australian all-rounder Keith Miller: 'I have seen other great knocks but, for my money, I rate his unbeaten 113 at Sabina Park against England in 1968 his finest.

'That Sabina Park pitch had giant-sized cracks – or should I say crevices – strewn cobweb-like throughout its 22 yard length as though some minor earth tremor had shaken Kingston. At this stage of the match, I examined the pitch and could insert all fingers of one hand, finger-length, into these huge cracks.

'It was a batsman's nightmare, especially for Sobers as he had been dismissed first ball in the first innings. Clive Lloyd had been bowled by John Snow with a shooter that not only cracked into the base of the stumps but had cut back some two feet from outside the off-stump. Clearly this was no pitch on which to play strokes but Sobers, grandly aided by Seymour Nurse, somehow dismissed the torments of the pitch from his mind and played strokes as though it was a plumb easy batting pitch.

'Frankly, this was the best innings in such atrocious conditions I have ever seen.'

(Reproduced from Sobers Benefit Tournament Souvenir Brochure, April 1973.)

18 Swing Against the Left

Rest of the World v England, Lord's, 1970

One of the favourite pastimes of any cricket-lover, of any age, is that of selection. We all feel that a better team could be chosen than the one in the field and selectors the world over have time and again felt the wrath of irate fans for their teams' defeats.

When I was a boy, we used to pretend we were picking a world team for some mythical match against the rest of the universe and it always provoked argument – and a lot of fun. We knew a world team couldn't be a reality and, in any case, selections were not affected by such considerations as injury or unavailability.

As it happens, several Rest of the World teams have been chosen for a variety of reasons since those days and I've been honoured to have captained two of them: those which replaced cancelled South African tours to England in 1970 and Australia in 1971–72. Kerry Packer also had a World team in his two seasons of World Series Cricket and when Barbados became independent in 1966 we had the temerity to take on a World team as part of the celebrations.

In almost every case, it was impossible to get together what could be considered the best team. Some players were unavailable, either because they were injured or because they were not interested. In the Barbados match, plans to include three South Africans – the Pollock brothers and Colin Bland – had to be abandoned because of political considerations and we ended up playing, and being badly beaten by, opponents hardly representative of the best of the rest. The

113

world team to Australia in 1971–72 was without several of the day's best players, as was Packer's World squad some years later.

There was one exception to this general rule, however, and it was in the very first series involving a World team against England in England in 1970. We had, as openers, Barry Richards and Eddie Barlow, both of whom were at the height of their powers then and who, along with some of the other outstanding South African players of the time, were to suffer badly from the international boycott which has kept South Africa out of Test cricket ever since. The Pollocks, Graeme the batsman and Peter the bowler, and the all-rounder Mike Procter, who later did so well for Gloucestershire, were the other South Africans in the team.

Let me say on the subject of South Africa that I am a sportsman and have always judged people as I have found them. To me, the colour of your skin, or what country you come from, doesn't matter. I have found that sport forms a common bond between all peoples and so it was with the South Africans with whom I played. This is not to say that I am completely insensitive to the political and moral issues involved but I sometimes wonder if the politicians cannot appreciate the value of sport in fostering international good-will between men. Certainly there was nothing but a tremendous feeling of camaraderie between the players who comprised those World teams – black and white; West Indian and South African; Australian and Indian; Pakistani and New Zealander.

In addition to Graeme Pollock, we had Rohan Kanhai, Clive Lloyd, Mushtaq Mohammed, and myself in the middle order; Procter and Intikhab Alam, the Pakistani leg-spinner, as top-class all-rounders, with a little help from Eddie Barlow and myself; Lance Gibbs as the off-spinner and Graham McKenzie, 'Big Garth', the Australian from Perth, or Peter Pollock to share the new ball with either myself or Procter, with Farouk Engineer of India and Deryck Murray to keep wicket.

Personally, I haven't played in any stronger team although I should make that statement conditional since we were not representing a country and the feeling of national identity so evident in Test cricket was, obviously, not present as it is in Test cricket. In fact, when the idea was raised of a World team playing a series of five Tests that summer, I turned down the invitation to play. Simply, I felt that it was being unfair to Nottinghamshire, for whom I had signed in 1968, who were paying me well for my services but who would again have to do without them for much of the season.

I'd enormously enjoyed my first season with the county in 1968, especially since we have moved from 15th in the table to fourth. I was confident we would do even better after that encouraging start but then I was with the West Indies on tour of England for half the 1969 season and now here was another series, for the second year in succession, which would mean that I'd yet again have to miss several matches for Notts.

In the end, the Test and County Cricket Board twisted the counties' arms a bit for the release of the overseas players and we all participated. I believe Guinness had put up a lot of sponsorship money, much of which went back into the counties, so there was a sort of *quid pro quo*.

Such an undertaking was an experiment and there were a lot of cynics who believed it would flop. There wouldn't be the Test match atmosphere, they said, even though the England players would earn caps. What is more, it was the summer of a general election, the World Cup soccer finals in Mexico and the Commonwealth Games in Edinburgh and it was difficult to compete for the public's attention with all this going on.

So it was a pleasant surprise to us all when the series turned out to be keenly contested, enjoyable and very popular, with a high standard of cricket played. The World team won the series 4–1 but it was not as lop-sided a result as it sounds. With the exception of the first, which we won by an innings, and the second, which England won by eight wickets to square the series, the matches were close. England's standard was lifted by playing such powerful opponents and I'm sure the preparation was ideal for their tour of Australia in the winter when Ray Illingworth's team recaptured the Ashes. For me personally, it was a grand summer for I did well with both bat and ball and the first match at Lord's is one which I'll always remember.

England went into the match without some of their top batsmen: Boycott, Cowdrey, Edrich, Graveney and Milburn were not in the side for one reason or another, which meant they had an inexperienced team – not the best formula against such opposition. Nor on such a pitch as this. I have never seen the ball move around like it did on that first day. I can't explain what caused it for the pitch looked no different from the usual Lord's strip, though perhaps a little greener. It was the day before the general election and all the pollsters were saying that the next government would be decided by the 'swinging voters'. There certainly was a lot of swinging at Lord's that morning and England soon found thcmselves 44 for seven, eventually reaching 127.

Usually at Lord's, where the ground is on a slope, I found I could get a ball to move away from the right-hander down the hill. It was not only doing that but also coming back up the slope! No wonder I had six for 21 off 20 overs when it was all over.

Luckily for us, we took a break for the people of Great Britain to vote on the second day – the Thursday – and this gave the pitch more time to lose its early moisture. By the time we came back, Ted Heath was the new Prime Minister, the Conservatives were in power and Harold Wilson was an ex-PM. One of the newspapers in the dressing room next day carried a headline 'Swing against the left!' and Farouk Engineer, never one to miss the chance of a pun, suggested that left-handers would struggle in future!

There were few of us shoring up our middle order and

117

when Graeme Pollock and Clive Lloyd were both bowled without amassing too many, Farouk quipped as I walked out of the dressing room: 'Swing against the left'! Whether Mr Wilson took any particular comfort from it, I'm rather doubtful, but I was 147 when I came back in at the end of the day. The pitch was now an absolute beauty and Lord's has always been a happy hunting ground for me. 'Swing back to the left,' I smiled at Farouk as I took my pads off.

Next day, I went for 183 and, ahead by over 400, we proceeded to win by an innings in spite of England's fighting second knock in which Ray Illingworth followed his 63 on the first day with a captain's 94. In fact, it looked at one stage as if we mightn't make it, with England over 300 with only five down. But then, on a slightly worn pitch, I joined Intikhab with some back-of-the-hand spin, had Illy picked up at slip off the googly and watched as Intikhab cleaned up the tail in quick order.

There were several outstanding performances later in the series and, just to prove that the election results had no bearing on the cricket, Clive Lloyd scored centuries at Trent Bridge and Edgbaston, I made another at Headingley and Graeme Pollock at last came good with a scintillating 114 in the final match at the Oval. Significantly, though, no *English* left-hander achieved anything!

English writer Gordon Ross: 'When Sobers ravaged the England batting on the first morning and finished with six for 21 in 20 overs, 11 of them maidens, and England had been shot out for 127, the Rest replying with 115 for 2 by the close, the game died as a competitive game of cricket. But it lived in mind and memory for some of the most glorious stroke-making by Sobers that Lord's has seen for years.

'Sobers made the ball move on that first morning more than I had seen it move at Lord's since Ian Thomson won the Gillette Cup for Sussex by destroying Warwickshire's early batting in the

Rest of the World v England, Lord's, 1970

England

B. W. Luckhurst	c Richards b Sobers	1	c Engineer b Intikhab	67
A. Jones	c Engineer b Procter	5	c Engineer b Procter	0
M. H. Denness	c Barlow b McKenzie	13	c Sobers b Intikhab	24
B. L. d'Oliveira	c Engineer b Sobers	0	c Lloyd b Intikhab	78
P. J. Sharpe	c Barlow b Sobers	4	b Sobers	2
R. Illingworth*	c Engineer b Sobers	63	c Barlow b Sobers	94
A. P. E. Knott†	c Kanhai b Sobers	2	lbw b Gibbs	39
J. A. Snow	c Engineer b Sobers	2	b Intikhab	10
D. L. Underwood	c Lloyd b Barlow	19	c Kanhai b Intikhab	7
A. Ward	c Sobers b McKenzie	11	st Engineer b Intikhab	0
K. Shuttleworth	not out	1	not out	0
Extras	(LB 5, NB 1)	6	(B 4, LB 8, NB 6)	18
Total		**127**		**339**

Rest of the World

B. A. Richards	c Sharpe b Ward	35
E. J. Barlow	c Underwood b Illingworth	119
R. B. Kanhai	c Knott b d'Oliveira	21
R. G. Pollock	b Underwood	55
C. H. Lloyd	b Ward	20
G. St A. Sobers*	c Underwood b Snow	183
F. M. Engineer†	b Ward	2
Intikhab Alam	b Ward	61
M. J. Procter	b Snow	26
G. D. McKenzie	c Snow b Underwood	0
L. R. Gibbs	not out	2
Extras	(B 10, LB 5, NB 7)	22
Total		**546**

Rest of the World	O	M	R	W		O	M	R	W
McKenzie	16.1	3	43	2		15	8	25	0
Procter	13	6	20	1		15	4	36	1
Sobers	20	11	21	6		31	13	43	2
Barlow	4	0	26	1		7	2	10	0
Intikhab	2	0	11	0		54	24	113	6
Lloyd						1	0	3	0
Gibbs						51	17	91	1

England	O	M	R	W
Snow	27	7	109	2
Ward	33	4	121	4
Shuttleworth	21	2	85	0
d'Oliveira	18	5	45	1
Underwood	25.5	8	81	2
Illingworth	30	8	83	1

1964 Final. Those quite close to Sobers had suggested that whilst his batting still burgeoned, his quick bowling was nothing like as effective as it used to be and he may not pay as much attention to that particular one of his many facets in the future. Sobers proved that this theory can be thrown to the four winds.'

(Reproduced from *Playfair Cricket Monthly*, August 1970.)

19 Reversing Lillee's Charges

Rest of the World v Australia, Melbourne, 1972

The decision by the South African government back in 1968 to bar Basil d'Oliveira from touring there with an MCC team has had its repercussions on world cricket ever since. The immediate effect was the cancellation of two planned South African tours, which led to their replacement by tours of Rest of the World teams. The first was to England in 1970 and the second to Australia in 1971–72. I had the honour to captain both.

It was a bold experiment and no one knew quite how the tours would be accepted by a public which regarded Test cricket as a contest only between countries. The Doubting Thomases felt the matches wouldn't have the same intense rivalry and would create little interest. They were proved wrong and both tours were outstanding successes. It was the first time cricket had known a team playing at this level with representatives from every country – including South Africa.

On both those tours, all of our players got on magnificently, on and off the field. We were a team and played as such and I forged many lasting friendships. To illustrate my point about the influence of sport I can relate a story. During both tours India and Pakistan were engaged in a bitter dispute which led to open warfare. Yet we had Pakistanis and Indians in our teams, and not only was there never any animosity between them, but they even got together to draft a message to their governments urging peace.

The 1970 team, I would say, was just about the best that could be assembled; the one which went to Australia the following year was not. Even so the Australians, who sponsored the tour and gathered the players together, still managed to attract some of the top names in the game – Kanhai, the Pollocks, Clive Lloyd, Zaheer Abbas, Gavaskar, Engineer. We were adequate in batting and spin-bowling but lacked genuine fast bowlers, which is a disadvantage in Australia.

I had really been looking forward to spending that season relaxing, perhaps playing some Sheffield Shield cricket for South Australia who had invited me back, I believe, as a sort of thank-you gesture for my time with them back in the 1960s. I'd had a demanding series against India in the Caribbean early in the year and this was followed by a full county season in which I skippered Nottinghamshire. I wasn't getting any younger and could have done with a rest, mentally as much as physically.

When Sir Donald Bradman telephoned, talked about the world team tour and asked me to lead the team, I was reluctant. But he's a persuasive talker and I had a great deal of respect for him. In the end, I found myself in Australia in late October as the multi-national force gathered.

The cynics, who doubted whether such an undertaking would be accepted by the Australian public, were nodding their heads and saying 'I told you so' by the time we were soundly beaten by an innings in the second 'Test' at Perth, only to be followed by an innings defeat at the hands of South Australia just before Christmas.

I was getting a lot of stick as well for my own lack of form and we were being told that we didn't care, that we were on a joy ride, and other rather uncomplimentary things. We were all desperately keen to silence such talk and, even though we were pretty ashamed of being skittled out for 59 in the first innings of the Perth 'Test', we knew we had collapsed on the lively Perth pitch to some of the fastest bowling we had ever seen. The bowler was a young tearaway by the name of Dennis Lillee. The world would hear a bit more of him in the years ahead.

I caught my first sight of Dennis in the first 'Test' at Brisbane. I was sitting next to Ray Lindwall at the time and my first comment concerned Lillee's run. 'Does this fellow really have to take such a long run?' I asked Ray. It took only two balls to see why he did for, even though the pitch was typically slow, there was no denying this boy had speed. If he kept this up, I wondered what would happen at Perth.

My worst fears were realized. When we arrived at the ground on the first morning, Richard Hutton dropped the ball onto the pitch and it bounced back up almost head high. 'If ah did that at Headingley ah'd have to get 'shovel to dig it out!' he said. We were forewarned. As I was the quickest bowler in the team we didn't have the resources to utilize this paceman's paradise. They did, with Lillee and Graham McKenzie. To add to our horror, the pitch sweated under the covers overnight and left some dampness in it when we started our innings on the second morning. Lillee tore through our batting, had eight for 20-odd and we were dismissed for 59 in less than 15 overs. I gloved a lifter, second ball, to Marsh behind the wicket, out for 0, and even though we did a lot better in the second innings, with a brilliant century from Rohan Kanhai, we returned east with our reputation in tatters.

The next match was at the Melbourne Cricket Ground, until then never my happy hunting ground. On my two tours with the West Indies and in my Sheffield Shield days for South Australia it was the only ground on which I had never made a century. It wasn't long before I was running true to form.

We were three down for next to nothing in the first innings when I came in to replace Graeme Pollock, who had just gone to Lillee. First ball, Dennis dropped it short and, probably conditioned by Perth, I played my stroke too soon and Keith Stackpole caught me down by his ankle in the slips. Out first ball – and to Lillee again.

In the dressing-room afterwards I told Ian Chappell, the Australian skipper, within Dennis' earshot: 'What's up with

123

this fellow, Ian? I've met him in three innings now and every time he's let me have a bouncer first up. Tell him I can bowl them too!' It was nothing more than a taunt and when Dennis did come in to bat at No. 11, the last thing on my mind was to give him a bouncer – until, that is, Tony Greig called from mid-on: 'Let him have it now; give him the bouncer.' By this time, Dennis was shaping pretty well so I considered Greig's advice was in order. Down came the bouncer and whizzed past Dennis's nose. It did the trick. He turned pink and next ball, just stood there and whacked it to be caught at mid off.

That set the cat among the pigeons! In the dressing-room, Ian Chappell said Dennis had been furious when he came in and had promised, I think the words were, 'to teach that cheeky bastard I haven't bowled at him yet'. It was fighting talk although I didn't need that to wake me up to the fact that I hadn't made a score so far on the tour. I was overdue.

I've never worried about failure too much because I feel it will come right in the end. In the preceding match, I'd made a century against Tasmania and knew there was basically nothing wrong with my form. When I went out to bat in the second innings, as fate would have it, Dennis Lillee was just taking the second new ball. It was the kind of confrontation which made the adrenalin pump and when I straight-drove his first ball to the boundary from the middle of the bat I felt that, somehow, this was going to be the innings when I broke that old Melbourne jinx. In three overs from Dennis and Bob Massie, in fact, I had 30 and by the end of the day had gone past the century mark.

The pitch was a beauty and everything went just right as almost every attacking shot found the gaps and went to the boundary. Lillee, and the swing bowler Massie, bowled a lot, as did the two leg-spinners in the side, Terry Jenner and Kerry O'Keeffe. Dennis, inexperienced as he was then, was bowling too short. The Sunday rest day gave us all time to relax but, since we were behind by about 100 on the first innings, I knew we needed to get a lot more when we resumed on the Monday.

Sometimes a break like that can completely ruin an innings so I began carefully before being convinced that I could open out again. I was lucky that Peter Pollock, at No. 9, kept his end up and together we added over 180 as we got into a winning position. Finally, at 254, I lifted a catch to long-on off Greg Chappell. There was a big crowd at the MCG that day, something over 50,000, as there had been on the Saturday, and at last I'd proven to Victorians that I could bat a bit.

Later there were some very flattering comments about my innings by people whose judgement I respect. The most flattering of all came from the greatest, the Don himself, who was kind enough to say it was probably the best-ever knock seen in Australia. He, of course, had played a few worthy ones in his time from what I can gather! I was especially touched when he gave the commentary for a film of the innings which was later distributed all over the world, and which I still show now and then at sports night functions – just for old time's sake!

Still, the compliment I remember most vividly came from Dennis Lillee, the young tyro, as I was walking in after my dismissal. He was applauding and when I passed him he said: 'You know I've read about you but now I've really seen you. We got our backsides cut good and proper today but I still appreciate it!' We'd been at each other ever since Perth, he had got me twice for ducks and now, at last, I had come out on top. His generous comment made me realize just what sport is all about.

Australian writer Ray Robinson: 'Looking for a double-century to compare to Gary Sobers' scintillating 254 for the World XI against Australia is like gazing at the Crown Jewels with the naked eye. The glitter almost makes my eyes water.

'Many say the matchless West Indian left-hander's batting delighted them more than any other innings they have watched. Test veterans of such standing as Sir Donald Bradman and W. J.

O'Reilly had to go back thirty-four years to Stan McCabe's unique 232 against England at Nottingham to recall an innings outshining it.

'Having seen the finest players of the last 50 years, Sir Donald said: 'I believe Sobers' was the greatest exhibition of batting seen in Australia. I have seen nothing to equal it in this country. Overseas, I still believe Stan McCabe's 232 at Nottingham was, in some respects, better.'

' . . . Batting as nobody else can, Sobers instantly took command. The captain's second shot was a hook and he sped to his first Melbourne 100 off 129 balls. In almost every over before Gary's arrival Lillee had looked like taking a wicket. Cuts began scudding past point so rapidly that a third-man posted almost square on the wide boundary could not intercept them.

'When Ian Chappell brought Lillee back with the second new ball Sobers defused the fast bowler's explosive attack. What appeared to be a length ball was driven straight to hit the sightscreen almost before Dennis had completed his follow-through. Challenging shots like that struck 29 off three overs from Lillee.'

(Reproduced from *The Cricketer*, March 1972.)

Rest of the World v Australia, Melbourne, 1971–72 (3rd Match)

World XI

H. M. Ackerman	b Lillee	0	c Stackpole b Lillee	9
S. M. Gavaskar	c G. S. Chappell b Lillee	38	c I. M. Chappell b Jenner	27
Zaheer Abbas	c Stackpole b Massie	4	c I. M. Chappell b Lillee	86
R. G. Pollock	c Marsh b Lillee	8	b Massie	28
G. St A. Sobers*	c Stackpole b Lillee	0	c Walters b G. S. Chappell	254
A. W. Greig	c Benaud b Massie	66	c and b Jenner	3
F. M. Engineer†	c Marsh b Lillee	5	b Lillee	14
Intikhab Alam	lbw b Jenner	38	lbw b Watson	15
P. M. Pollock	lbw b Jenner	3	c O'Keeffe b Jenner	54
N. Gifford	not out	0	not out	4
B. S. Bedi	run out	7	c Massie b Jenner	3
Extras	(B 5, LB 8, W 1, NB 1)	15	(LB 13, W 3, NB 1)	17
Total		**184**		**514**

Australia

K. R. Stackpole	c Ackerman b Greig	32	c Engineer b Greig	24
G. D. Watson	c R. G. Pollock b Greig	16	retired hurt	21
I. M. Chappell*	b P. M. Pollock	21	run out	41
J. Benaud	lbw b Intikhab	24	c Sobers b Intikhab	42
G. S. Chappell	not out	115	c Sobers b Bedi	12
K. D. Walters	b Greig	16	c sub b Bedi	127
R. W. Marsh†	b Greig	4	lbw b Bedi	0
K. J. O'Keeffe	c Gavaskar b Intikhab	1	c Sobers b Intikhab	1
T. J. Jenner	c Engineer b Sobers	19	c Gavaskar b Bedi	12
R. A. L. Massie	c Engineer b Sobers	34	c and b Intikhab	23
D. K. Lillee	c Bedi b Sobers	0	not out	1
Extras	(B 1, LB 2)	3	(B 6, LB 2, W 1, NB 4)	13
Total		**285**		**317**

Australia	O	M	R	W	O	M	R	W
Lillee	16.3	4	48	5	30	3	133	3
Massie	14	3	70	2	25	4	95	1
Chappell	10	2	17	0	3	1	12	1
Watson	3	1	10	0	16	2	37	1
Jenner	6	0	24	2	20.3	5	87	4
Walters					2	0	5	0
O'Keeffe					27	5	121	0
Stackpole					1	0	7	0
World XI								
Pollock	19	2	87	1	1	0	8	0
Sobers	14.6	0	16	3	8	0	48	0
Greig	16	4	41	4	14	1	71	1
Intikhab	12	0	45	2	24	5	83	3
Bedi	6	0	28	0	24	4	81	4
Gifford	4	0	14	0	5	1	13	0

20 Lifting the Curse of the Kiwis

West Indies v New Zealand, Bridgetown, 1972

Most cricketers have their particular bogey team or ground. My jinx was New Zealand, where on two tours and in seven Tests I did not pass 50 once and had never taken more than a handful of wickets. My first Test against New Zealand was in 1956 and I had to wait sixteen long years before I did anything of note against them.

New Zealand, in fact, was my first overseas tour. That year, 1956, the West Indies picked a team somewhat below full strength whilst including several promising young players. I just about knew where New Zealand was on the map; we had learned at school that it produced a whole lot of sheep and I'd read about their cricketers in the newspapers. Apart from that, I really didn't know what to expect.

I certainly didn't expect it to be coldest place I've ever played cricket. We had a match at a venue called Invercargill and you could believe them when they said there was no town in the world closer to the South Pole. It was freezing! What is more, the pitches came as a shock to all of us who had been brought up in the West Indies on grassless, hard, flat surfaces. By comparison, pitches in New Zealand looked like strips of rough ground and I believe I psyched myself out after one look at them. 'How can I bat on these?' I asked myself. The answer was, simply, that I couldn't because I didn't have the confidence. Yet Everton Weekes seemed to find no difficulty as he reeled off four consecutive centuries in the four Tests. It was all in the mind and I ended the series with less than 100 runs – all told!

The West Indies returned to New Zealand twelve years later and, by then, I was captain. The tour was tacked on at the end of an exhausting and very disappointing series of five Tests in Australia which we lost 3–1, and we were a dis-spirited side by the time we left Sydney for Auckland in early February. Neither the weather nor the cricketing conditions had changed much in New Zealand in the intervening years and, what with the disappointment over the loss in Australia, I don't think we were in the right frame of mind to tackle the three Tests against a keen and well-balanced New Zealand team itching to prove itself. We had to share the series with one of each – a win, a loss and a draw – and again yours truly had a miserable time with bat and ball: again fewer than 100 runs all told and a handful of wickets.

By the time New Zealand came to the West Indies on their first tour in 1972 I was honestly wondering whether I'd been blighted against them. I had done well against every Test-playing country and *in* every Test-playing country and it was not as if their cricket, for all its spirited application, was all that strong. It just had to be a jinx!

Nothing that happened in the first two Tests of that series served to remove my doubts. Lawrence Rowe, that incredibly gifted batsman with a beautiful sense of timing and balance, made his dream debut to Test cricket with a double century followed by a single in the Test at Sabina Park but we still had to settle for a draw.

In the second at the Queen's Park Oval in Port-of-Spain, I won the toss and decided to send them in. They were six down before reaching 100 but then we dropped eight – yes, eight – catches, they recovered and again we played out a draw. Surely now, I had to believe I had been struck by some particular Kiwi curse!

By now, the West Indian public and press were becoming agitated at our inability to break through. We had not won a Test for some time and had lost to the Indians the year before. The fact is, our great team of the 1960s had broken up and we were trying to rebuild. Even Rohan Kanhai and

129

Lance Gibbs, who were still in the game and who were to return to make such a vital contribution later, were unavailable for that series.

Would my luck against the New Zealanders ever change? If anything, it became even worse at the start of the third Test in Barbados. I had always known the pitch at Kensington Oval to contain a little life early on, yet it had never been anything but an ideal batting surface and the captain winning the toss there would have been mad not to have batted first. The Indian skipper, Ajit Wadekar, had discovered this the previous season when he sent us in and we proceeded to pile up over 500 for five declared.

So when I won the toss I told Bev Congdon, who had taken over as New Zealand captain from the injured Graham Dowling: 'We'll bat.' But the jinx was on me again. This time I'd misread the pitch which I thought I knew so well. True, there was a little more green in it than usual but I never expected it to seam around as it did and big Bruce Taylor, a more-than-useful bowler at fast-medium delivering from a height, made fullest use of the conditions. We were something like 50 for six in no time and were all out for 133 with big Bruce, who enjoyed a wonderful tour, taking seven.

By this time, the sun had taken whatever life there was out of the pitch and New Zealand proceeded to score over 400, with centuries from Congdon and Bruce Hastings. We were behind by almost 300 on the first innings, there was loads of time left and the old New Zealand evil eye was focusing on what looked, for the West Indies, like a very embarrassing defeat. It was, I can admit, a most uncomfortable feeling when I went out in our second innings with five wickets down and still over 100 runs in arrears.

By now, the New Zealanders must really have been saying to themselves: 'This fellow Sobers is running scared of us. Here he is, coming in at No. 7.' The reason was that I'd used Mike Findlay, our wicket-keeper, as nightwatchman the evening before but it meant that there was not much left to come after Charlie Davis and myself, the sixth-wicket pair and the last of the specialist batsmen. Those who had criticized me all along for batting too low in the order at No. 6 were having a field day.

Yet I had never run out of partners before and, to my great relief, I didn't now. Charlie was always a very gritty fighter and as good a man to have in a crisis as any. The tougher the situation, the better he seemed to play – and this was how he dedicated himself now. While he kept up his concentration and application for hour after hour at one end, I finally finished off the New Zealand bogey which had plagued me since 1956.

There was even a touch of the supernatural about the whole business. I was on 87, that figure which Australians regard so suspiciously because it is 13 short of the century, when I slashed at Bruce Taylor and edged a catch straight into Terry Jarvis's lap at first slip. Amazingly, he dropped it. The jinx was finally and at last laid to rest with that one stroke of luck and I went on to finish with 142. Charlie, never flustered, kept on picking up his runs, 183 of them, and we easily saved the game in the end. Our sixth-wicket partnership was worth 254 when Graham Vivian, one of the finest fielders I have ever seen and who excelled in that series, swooped on a firm, low hook stroke off the second new ball to make a stunning catch off Taylor.

It happened to be the one-and-only century I ever scored against New Zealand and it completed a satisfying record of having registered one against every Test-playing country. More than that, however, it saved the match for the West Indies – and saw off that worrying bogey.

The West Indies Cricket Annual, 1972: 'When Sobers joined Davis it seemed he had left his entrance until too late. Only the unpredictable Holford and the three bowlers were to follow, at least 9½ hours' playing time remained and West Indies were still 118 in arrears. Already, too, Davis, then 18, had given Turner an easy slip chance cutting at Howarth – subsequently to prove a very important error.

'As it turned out, Sobers found the type of partner he had done so often in the past in his many rescue acts for the West Indies. With neither batsman taking the slightest risk the West Indies reached 297 without further loss by the close of play.

'There was the whole of the rest day to consider the prospects and, although the position was still very much in favour of a New Zealand victory, Barbadians showed their confidence in Sobers and, to a lesser extent, Davis by packing the ground on the last day. The crowd of approximately 12,000 was the largest for the last day of a Test in Kensington's history.

'New Zealand had one great opportunity of separating the partnership before the match was safe for the West Indies but let it slip. After half an hour, Sobers (87) slashed at a ball from Taylor and top-edged a catch straight to Jarvis at first slip who dropped it. At that stage, the West Indies lead was a mere 32. By the time Sobers was well taken at square leg off Taylor's bowling with the third new ball, it was 136 and the result was virtually decided.'

West Indies v New Zealand, Bridgetown, 1971–72 (3rd Test)

West Indies

R. C. Fredericks	c Hastings b Cunis	5	lbw b Cunis	28
M. C. Carew	c Morgan b Taylor	1	c Turner b Howarth	45
L. G. Rowe	c Wadsworth b Taylor	0	lbw b Congdon	51
C. A. Davis	c Jarvis b Taylor	1	run out (5)	183
G. St A. Sobers*	c Wadsworth b Congdon	35	c Vivian b Taylor (7)	142
M. L. C. Foster	c Wadsworth b Taylor	22	lbw b Taylor	4
D. A. J. Holford	c Wadsworth b Taylor	3	c Wadsworth b Congdon (8)	50
T. M. Findlay†	not out	44	c Morgan b Howarth (4)	9
Inshan Ali	b Taylor	3	not out	12
V. A. Holder	b Congdon	3	not out	16
G. C. Shillingford	c Morgan b Taylor	15		
Extras	(NB 1)	1	(B 6, LB 9, W 1, NB 8)	24
Total		**133**	(8 wickets)	**564**

New Zealand

G. M. Turner	c Holford b Holder	21
T. W. Jarvis	lbw b Shillingford	26
B. E. Congdon*	lbw b Holder	126
M. G. Burgess	c Fredericks b Sobers	19
B. F. Hastings	lbw b Sobers	105
R. W. Morgan	c Fredericks b Ali	2
G. E. Vivian	b Sobers	38
K. J. Wadsworth†	not out	15
B. R. Taylor	lbw b Sobers	0
R. S. Cunis	c Findlay b Holder	27
H. J. Howarth	b Shillingford	8
Extras	(LB 13, NB 22)	35
Total		**422**

New Zealand	O	M	R	W		O	M	R	W
Cunis	10	3	26	1		38	8	130	1
Taylor	20.3	6	74	7		33	3	108	2
Congdon	16	3	26	2		31	7	66	2
Howarth	3	1	6	0		74	24	138	2
Morgan						30	8	78	0
Vivian						8	2	20	0

West Indies	O	M	R	W
Holder	40	13	91	3
Sobers	29	6	64	4
Shillingford	24.2	7	65	2
Davis	10	3	19	0
Ali	35	11	81	1
Holford	9	0	20	0
Foster	14	2	40	0
Fredericks	2	0	7	0

21 On My Last Leg at Lord's

West Indies v England, Lord's, 1973

There is something of a story behind my final Test series in England and, while it was not a particularly pleasant one, it did have a happy ending, with a century in the last innings I ever played at Lord's, so I'll tell it nevertheless.

After so many years of almost continuous cricket all over the world, it was not surprising that some part of my overworked body should rebel. In the summer of 1972, after two tough, back-to-back series for Rest of the World in Australia and the West Indies against New Zealand in the Caribbean, I returned to Nottinghamshire and soon realized that I couldn't play on with an increasingly painful right knee.

It was that dreaded problem all sportsmen fear, a damaged cartilage, and the doctors were performing the operation for its removal before the end of the season. I was particularly disappointed because it meant that yet again I would not be able to play for a full season with Nottinghamshire, who had been so good to me since I first joined them in 1968 but who had to put up with my lengthy absences, playing for the West Indies and skippering the Rest of the World side.

I also realized then that my position as West Indies captain for the series against Australia, scheduled early in 1973, was in doubt. I was then thirty-six years of age and I wasn't going to fool myself that there would be any magical formula to bring me back to full fitness in a twinkling. So I gave the West Indies Board ample notice of my position, resigned as captain and was succeeded by Rohan Kanhai, a player of tremendous experience and a good reader of the game.

The Board offered to bring me home, at its own expense, for the Australian series, an offer extended to all those who were playing county cricket at the time and who, it felt, would be needed for the West Indies team. However, I couldn't know then whether I would be fit in time to participate in the series, so I told them I'd pay my own passage back and, if I were fit enough to play, would then expect to be reimbursed.

So I duly returned to Barbados and started the process of getting that knee back in working order, mainly using weight training. I was desperately keen to play against the Australians; after the series against them for the Rest of the World a year earlier I knew their strength. Their performance in England in the summer, with Dennis Lillee, Bob Massie and Greg Chappell coming to the fore, warned us what to expect.

A couple of weeks before the first Test in Jamaica Clyde Walcott, who was one of the selectors, called me and asked how I felt. 'To tell the truth, I feel as if I could play in Jamaica,' I told him, only half-jokingly. But I told him not to consider me even though I was really pleased with the way the knee was progressing. I would have to put it to the test first, I was told. So I did. Barbados were playing their final match in the Shell Shield that season against Trinidad and Tobago at the Queen's Park Oval, always a needle match between long-standing arch-rivals, and Barbados would retain the Shield if we won. It came between the first and second Tests, so the timing was perfect when David Holford, the Barbados skipper, asked me after a net session one afternoon if I felt fit enough to play. By now, I was sure I was ready for a four-day match and I was glad of the opportunity to get back into the game.

I didn't exactly set Trinidad on fire, getting 20 or so in each innings and bowling about 20 overs in the match. Also, the Trinidadians beat us. But at least I'd proven to myself that I was ready to return. I didn't leave the field once and even used the new ball in the first innings.

Afterwards Jeff Stollmeyer, chairman of the selectors' panel at the time, came into the dressing room and asked: 'How's it going, Gary? Any after-effects?' Well, in my first match after the operation, doctors had told me to expect swelling and a bit of stiffness and this is exactly what happened. I told Jeff as much, but said I was sure I'd be ready for the second Test in Barbados. Apparently, though, the selectors wanted me to play in the Aussies' match against Barbados just prior to the Test as further proof of my recovery and they also asked for the Board's doctor to conduct a fitness test.

Now this really got my back up. I had worked very hard to get back into shape, my own doctor had advised that it would be all right to play and yet the Board wouldn't accept my word. In the past, I had played for the West Indies with a strained muscle and with a septic finger *against* doctor's orders because the captain wanted me to play and because I assured him I was well enough. There had been no talk of fitness tests then.

I felt I'd been slighted – especially when they told me I had to play in a two-day practice match with the rest of the Test team in St Vincent between the second and third Tests. I'd given my heart for West Indies cricket for almost twenty years and didn't feel I had ever let them down. Why the selectors should have doubted my honesty now I'd never know. But that was it. I never did get the medical certificate they required and I never played in the series.

As you can imagine, the whole episode was not a pleasant experience and it stirred up a lot of controversy in the West Indies. One Barbadian parliamentarian put in his two cents worth by claiming that, even on one leg, I was better than most of the others, which may have sounded very complimentary, but which, I thought, missed the point. If I had been on one leg, I would have said so. But I knew I was fit enough. Dr Eric Williams, the Prime Minister of Trinidad and Tobago, was most upset by the whole thing and complained that I'd been tossed aside 'like an old car'. To be honest, that was how I felt.

It was my benefit season in Barbados and towards the end

of the Australian tour a special limited-overs tournament did give me the chance to show the Barbadian public at least that I wasn't trying to pull a fast one over my fitness earlier on. They really were wonderful and the benefit fund, organized by Banks, the brewéry in Barbados, raised a most welcome $85,000 – something like £18,000 at the time.

Immediately after that Australian series, the West Indies were scheduled for a shared tour of England in the latter half of the season. Before I returned to England to rejoin Notts, I was asked by the West Indies if I'd be available for their tour. I would be the first to admit that I was still smarting from my treatment over my fitness in the Australian series, especially since the West Indies lost 2–0. It wasn't to say that we were badly outplayed all the way through. Far from it. The third Test was a really close one and I'm sure I could have contributed something to the effort, had I been allowed to.

Now I was being asked to take part in another series, without any medical certificate, just a few months afterwards. Call that logic! But the proposition did pose a real dilemma. On the one hand, I have never been one to bear a grudge and I have always remained committed to West Indies cricket. If I was wanted, I would play. On the other hand, however, Nottinghamshire deserved better than I had been able to give them in all my time with them. I honestly felt that I could not leave them yet again for most of the season.

So I struck a compromise. I told the West Indies Board I would be available – but only for the three Tests. I would be playing county cricket for Notts and they would have to judge my fitness and form on the strength of that and decide if I was required.

Early in the tour, Esmond Kentish, a big but soft-spoken man who had been a fine fast bowler for Jamaica in his heyday, rang and asked: 'Gary, what's the position? Do you want to play?' 'No, Esmond, you've got it wrong,' I told him. 'It's a question of whether you require me to play. If you pick me, I'll play and I can promise you I'll give 100 per cent effort.'

So that was how I got back into the West Indies team and I can tell you I did feel the pressure early on to prove myself. I knew the doubters would be watching very keenly to see whether I would limp around the field like the cripple I was purported to be, anxious to know whether the old man had really gone.

By the time we reached the first Test at the Oval, however, I was having no trouble at all with the knee, although I hadn't exactly had a purple patch with either bat or ball in my matches for Nottinghamshire. As it turned out, my form gradually got better and better, so that I'd scored 10 (run out) and 51 in the first Test and 21 and 74 in the second at Edgbaston, in addition to picking up a few useful wickets in both matches as we moved on to Lord's for the third and final Test.

As you may have gathered by now, Lord's is one of my favourite places. Not for nothing is it called the headquarters of cricket. You can feel the great tradition all around you from the time you walk through the Grace Gates. I think you only have to walk down the staircase from the dressing room, through the Long Room and onto the hallowed turf before a big crowd to know that you're going to make runs. In my very first match there in 1957 I'd made a century for the West Indies against the MCC and in 1966 had shared that record match-saving partnership with David Holford which I still consider my best Test innings.

I never think about these things in the heat of a match but I suppose it was in the back of my mind that this was going to be my last Test in England – and at Lord's too. The sun shone from first to last, huge crowds were there and Rohan won the toss on a beautiful batting pitch. What more could I have asked for, except perhaps that the total be over 200 when I came in.

In fact, it was 256 for four when I joined Rohan, the two 'old men' of West Indies cricket together and both enjoying it immensely. The occasion was even more significant for Rohan than for me. I'm sure he felt, too, that this was his last Test in England, for we were not due back for another four years. What is more, he had never had a century at Lord's and, since we were ahead 1–0 entering that match, he wanted to ensure that we would clinch the series.

Rohan was in dazzling form that day, batting with superb timing and confidence in a tremendous innings of 157. He was out early on the second morning but he had taken the sting out of the England attack and next day myself and young Bernard Julien benefited. Julien, at the time, was a most promising all-round cricketer, a fine athlete who swung the ball about at left-arm medium fast, a brilliant fielder and right-handed batsman who hit the ball hard and cleanly. He had such a bright future that it was a great disappointment to me that he didn't carry on to greater things.

That day, he came in when I was well set and hit the ball from the middle of the bat right away. It was one of those situations when the poor fielding team can do little about events and we both went on to our hundreds so that we finished with 652 for eight before Rohan declared.

We proceeded to win by an innings and 226 runs, one of our biggest victories ever in Test cricket; England batted in both their innings like a team demoralized, which was no more than to be expected with such a huge total facing them. Perhaps the straw that broke the camel's back was Rohan's decision to keep on batting as long as he did – and to send me back in with the total on 604 for seven after I'd retired earlier with stomach cramps.

Ray Illingworth was England's captain, a tough Yorkshireman who lost the job to Mike Denness after our triumph in that series. Like any Yorkshireman, Ray doesn't give up easily but I'll never forget the expression of sheer disbelief on his face when I walked back out to bat that day! Just for good measure, I managed to hang on to six catches in the match – four in the slips and two round the corner off Lance Gibbs

England v West Indies, Lord's, 1973 (3rd Test)

West Indies

R. C. Fredericks	c Underwood b Willis	51
D. L. Murray†	b Willis	4
R. B. Kanhai*	c Greig b Willis	157
C. H. Lloyd	c and b Willis	63
A. I. Kallicharran	c Arnold b Illingworth	14
G. St A. Sobers	not out	150
M. L. C. Foster	c Willis b Greig	9
B. D. Julien	c and b Greig	121
K. D. Boyce	c Amiss b Greig	36
V. A. Holder	not out	23
L. R. Gibbs	did not bat	
Extras	(B 1, LB 14, W 1, NB 8)	24
Total	(8 wickets declared)	**652**

England

G. Boycott	c Kanhai b Holder	4	c Kallicharran b Boyce	15
D. L. Amiss	c Sobers b Holder	35	c Sobers b Boyce	10
B. W. Luckhurst	c Murray b Boyce	1	c Sobers b Julien (4)	12
F. C. Hayes	c Fredericks b Holder	8	c Holder b Boyce (5)	0
K. W. R. Fletcher	c Sobers b Gibbs	68	not out (6)	86
A. W. Greig	c Sobers b Boyce	44	lbw b Julien (7)	13
R. Illingworth*	c Sobers b Gibbs	0	c Kanhai b Gibbs (8)	13
A. P. E. Knott†	c Murray b Boyce	21	c Murray b Boyce (3)	5
G. G. Arnold	c Murray b Boyce	5	c Fredericks b Gibbs	1
R. G. D. Willis	not out	5	c Fredericks b Julien	0
D. L. Underwood	c Gibbs b Holder	12	b Gibbs	14
Extras	(B 6, LB 4, W 3, NB 17)	30	(B 9, W 1, NB 14)	24
Total		**233**		**193**

England	O	M	R	W	O	M	R	W
Arnold	35	6	111	0				
Willis	35	3	118	4				
Greig	33	2	180	3				
Underwood	34	6	105	0				
Illingworth	31.4	3	114	1				

West Indies								
Holder	15	3	56	4	14	4	18	0
Boyce	20	7	50	4	16	5	49	4
Julien	11	4	26	0	18	2	69	3
Gibbs	18	3	39	2	13.3	3	26	3
Sobers	8	0	30	0	4	1	7	0
Foster	1	0	2	0				

– which equalled the Test record. So, all in all, my Test finale at Lord's was quite something – and not bad for a 'one-legged' man unfit to play a few months earlier.

The Cricketer Quarterly, Autumn 1973: 'Of the three West Indian centuries, that which probably gave the most pleasure was the 150 not out by Sobers – this great cricketer, because of physical handicap, supposed to be beyond his best, showing that even on one leg, he remains among the 'Greats'. It was inspiring cricket and showed the affection in which Sobers is held the world over.'